APPRENTICED TO CHRIST

ACTIVITIES FOR
PRACTICING THE CATHOLIC WAY OF LIFE

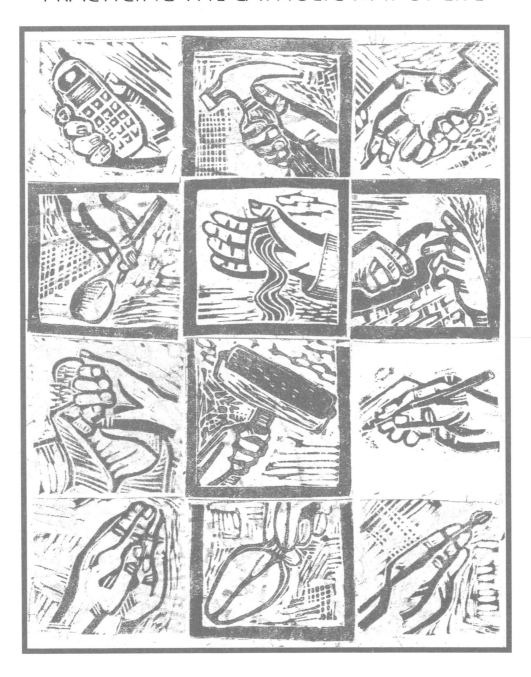

APPRENTICED to CHRIST

Activities for Practicing the Catholic Way of Life

Author: Jerry Galipeau, D. Min.
Editor: Michael E. Novak
Copy Editor: Marcia T. Lucey
Cover and Book Design: Chris Broquet
Editorial Director: Mary Beth Kunde-Anderson
Production Manager: Deb Johnston
Art: Paula Wendland

WLP 017266
ISBN 978-1-58459-327-0

017266

World Library Publications
the music and liturgy division of J.S. Paluch Company, Inc.
3708 River Road, Suite 400
Franklin Park, Illinois 60131-2158
800 566-6150
wlpcs@jspaluch.com • www.wlpmusic.com

CONTENTS

INTRODUCTION

An Experience That Changed Me

In the early 1990s, during my first year as director of liturgy and music at St. Marcelline Parish in Schaumburg, Illinois, I was put in charge of the parish's visit to our "sharing" parish, Our Lady of Lourdes, in the inner city of Chicago. I reserved two school buses and prepared the parish choir to sing at a Sunday morning Mass at Our Lady of Lourdes. When the morning of the visit arrived I was surprised to see the parish's director of Christian initiation coming toward one of the school buses with the catechumens and candidates in tow. I wondered aloud whether or not there would be a dismissal of catechumens at our sharing parish and just what the director planned on doing for their "session." She calmly told me to relax. We boarded the buses and headed into the city, through some of the poorest neighborhoods in Chicago.

When we arrived we discovered that the church's furnace was not functioning. It was November and the temperature hovered in the upper forties. It was quite cold in the old stone church. Some of the choir members wore their coats beneath their choir robes. We celebrated a wonderful Mass and were later treated to a delicious breakfast in the parish hall.

A week later our catechumens and candidates announced that they were starting a coat drive for the children of Our Lady of Lourdes. During the visit they noticed many of the parish's children in short-sleeve T-shirts. They wondered what would happen when the bitter Chicago winter weather arrived. They decided, on their own, and without the pastoral staff's "permission," that a coat drive was needed. In order to do this, they needed to learn how to get an article into the bulletin about the coat drive. They needed to learn how to arrange for announcements from the pulpit. They needed to secure a room in the parish center to collect and store the coats. They needed to schedule times for the drop-offs. In other words, they needed to learn, firsthand, what it meant to be a Catholic, a person who is Christ for others. Many on the parish staff and initiation team wondered if these catechumens and candidates would have been moved to initiate a justice project like the coat drive if, instead of going to the sharing parish, they were given a lecture on the Church's social ministry. We thought not.

◆

The Catechumenate as an Apprenticeship

This experience is an illustration of what this book is all about. This is a book about apprenticing people to the Catholic way of life. Apprenticeship is not a new way of formation. The Second Vatican Council, in paragraph 14 of its Decree on the Church's Missionary Activity, *Ad Gentes*, put forth the generating vision for the way that catechumens should be initiated.

> Those who, through the Church, have accepted from God a belief in Christ should be admitted to the catechumenate by liturgical rites. The catechumenate is not a mere expounding of doctrines and precepts, but a training period for the whole Christian life. It is an apprenticeship of appropriate length, during which disciples are joined to Christ their Teacher. Therefore, catechumens should be properly instructed in the mystery of salvation and in the practice of gospel morality. By sacred rites which are to be held at successive intervals, they should be introduced into the life of faith, liturgy, and love, which God's People lives.

This generating vision, that the catechumenate "is an apprenticeship of appropriate length, during which disciples are joined to Christ their Teacher" has not, at least in this author's experience, had its intended effect on the implementation of the Rite of Christian Initiation of Adults across the United States and Canada. An Internet search on the words "RCIA program" reveals that most RCIA programs are made up of a syllabus of topics designed to cover a range of Catholic doctrinal elements. In other words, it seems that what the Rite of Christian Initiation of Adults has turned into, in many places, is precisely what the generating vision of *Ad Gentes* warned against: "a mere expounding of doctrines and precepts." Most parishes celebrate the rites, and some programs are peppered with a limited amount of apostolic activity and connections with the parish community. For the majority of initiation programs, however, the expounding of doctrines and precepts remains at the core. Apprenticeship to the Christian life appears to be missing.

The *Rite of Christian Initiation of Adults*, in paragraph 75, takes up the generating vision of *Ad Gentes* and describes four ways to train people in the Christian way of life. They have been described in these general terms: catechesis, community, liturgy, and apostolic service. Throughout the United States and Canada, we have become quite good at the first of the four. There are all kinds of catechetical programs that assist initiation ministers in handing on the content of the Catholic faith. This book is intended to help initiation practitioners implement more fully the rest of paragraph 75's four-pillared approach to Christian formation.

The *General Directory for Catechesis*

Paragraph 67 of the *General Directory for Catechesis* speaks of the "fundamental characteristics of initiatory catechesis" in this way: "This comprehensive formation includes more than instruction: it is an apprenticeship of the entire Christian life." Paragraph 66 of the same document defines the aim of catechetical activity. "The aim of catechetical activity consists precisely in this: to encourage a living, explicit and fruitful profession of faith" (Cf. *Catechism of the Catholic Church* 1229; Second Vatican Council, *Decree on the Pastoral Office of Bishops in the Church*, Christus Dominus 14). The challenge posed to ministers of Christian initiation, as well as to all who are involved in the Church's catechetical ministry, is this: How do we transform initiation models that focus almost entirely on teaching dogma and precepts into models that embrace apprenticeship as the key generating vision? In other words, how do we move our formation processes in a direction that more fully encourages "a living, explicit, and fruitful profession of faith"?

The *National Directory for Catechesis*

Paragraph 29.G of the *National Directory for Catechesis*, published by the United States Conference of Catholic Bishops in 2005, expands on the apprenticeship model.

> In addition, learning by Christian living is an essential component of catechetical methodology. The active participation of all the catechized in their Christian formation fosters learning by doing. As a general condition of Christian life, the faithful actively respond to God's loving initiative through praying; celebrating the sacraments and the Liturgy; living the Christian life; fostering works of charity (meeting the needs of those who are poor and vulnerable) and works of justice (working to address the injustices that exist in the systemic and institutional organizations of society); and promoting virtues from the natural law such as liberty, solidarity, justice, peace, and the protection of the created order. The participation of adults in their own catechetical formation is essential, since they have the fullest capacity to understand the truths of the faith and live the Christian life.

The bishops are clear: "Learning by doing" is at the core of Christian formation and catechesis. What a wonderful way to embrace the call to catechize others! Often dubbed "boring" or "too intellectual," formation in the Christian way of life is not at all passive when it embraces the model of apprenticeship. Real live Christians doing Christ's work on this earth guide others in the actual doing of this work by showing them how their hands, feet, and voices become the hands, feet, and voice of Christ here and now. The bishops continue in paragraph 29.H: "It is a guided encounter with the entire Christian life, a journey toward conversion to Christ. It is a school for discipleship that promotes an authentic following of Christ."

Conversion at the Core

Conversion is at the center of the Church's catechetical and evangelical activity. Several years ago while I was working at a parish in central Florida, we invited our catechumens and candidates to prepare and serve the evening meal at the Orlando Coalition for the Homeless. That year one man, I'll call him Jack, was one of our catechumens. He was always ready to answer questions when asked. He was gregarious and would get more reticent catechumens and candidates involved in our faith conversations. After we staffed that meal for the poor, Jack became quite sullen and despondent over the next weeks. We asked his sponsor if Jack had become ill or had received bad news. The sponsor told us that Jack was doing fine and that he would let us know what was happening in due time. At a session weeks later, in the middle of a talk on some aspect of Catholic doctrine, Jack raised his hand and said, "I need to say something." He went on, "All of you remember the night we were feeding the poor at the Coalition for the Homeless. And, no doubt, you noticed that I was right on the front lines. I didn't want to be back in the kitchen making the Sloppy Joes. I didn't want to be on the set-up or tear-down crew. I wanted to be front and center, actually handing the food to the people. So there

I was, being handed a plate with some salad and an open hamburger bun on it. My job was to scoop the ladle into the mix and plop the Sloppy Joe mix onto the hamburger bun, then hand the plate to the poor person. Since there were hundreds that we were feeding that night, I kind of got into a rhythm–picking up the plate, scooping the mix with the ladle, plopping the mix onto the bun, serving the plate to the hungry person. All of a sudden it really dawned on me. *This* is what my hands were created to do–picking, scooping, plopping, and serving. My hands were created to feed hungry people." Jack then shared with the entire group the fact that for most of his adult life he had struggled with pornography. He told us that he couldn't believe what his hands had actually done in the past. He told us about his hands flipping through dirty magazines. He told us about his hands grasping remote control devices to watch filthy movies. He told us how his hands forked over lots of money to buy all this trash. Then he said, "That was *not* what my hands were meant to do. This is what my hands were meant to do." At that point he made the motions of picking, scooping, plopping, and serving. "*This*," he said, "*this* is what my hands were created to do."

Apprenticeship activities lead people to do what Jesus Christ would do. And when people become involved in the work of Christ, suddenly those things about their attitudes and actions that are least Christlike are set in stark relief. Jack was experiencing deep conversion, not because he was told what his hands were created to do, but because that telling was accompanied by actually *doing* what his hands were created to do.

The Apprenticeship Methodology

For years catechists have looked to the Sunday readings and the liturgical year in order to cull from these sources links to Catholic doctrine. This book does something similar. It examines the Sunday readings of the three years that make up our liturgical cycle with a view toward finding the kind of Christian action they might inspire. A particular line from the first reading, responsorial psalm, second reading, or Gospel forms the basis for inspiring an "apprenticeship activity." Following the suggested apprenticeship activity, the aspect of Christian formation to which the activity is related is identified. Then a list of primary catechetical resources is given, including pertinent paragraphs from the *Catechism of the Catholic Church*, the *United States Catholic Catechism for Adults*, papal and episcopal materials, and useful Web sites for more information and resources. The catechist can choose to refer to only these resources or supplement them from the wealth of catechetical materials that are available.

The movements of this formational process are Word→ Apprenticeship Activity→Mystagogical Catechesis. In other words, the scripture inspires Catholic doing and the role

of traditional catechesis comes in only after the "doing" of the Catholic activity. In this way, the catechetical resources function not in a vacuum, but within the context of lived faith. Catholic tradition is an important conversation partner with the actual Catholic activity. A section detailing how to apply this catechetical method is provided on page 8.

Obviously each Sunday's set of scripture readings can inspire many apprenticeship activities. They also inspire a myriad of catechetical approaches. The apprenticeship activities suggested here are some among many. Given the time constraints of so many in our initiation processes, it would be highly improbable that an initiation process could be structured solely around these activities. This book is meant as a resource to help initiation ministers weave apprenticeship activities into their current way of initiating new Catholics. This book suggests an apprenticeship activity inspired by the readings for each Sunday. For initiation processes that are topically driven rather than driven by the Sunday word, an index of topics is given. Find the topic, then the Sunday(s) listed under that topic. For these Sundays, an apprenticeship activity is suggested that is connected to that topic.

Some parishes will find a multitude of possibilities when it comes to connecting those in the initiation process with the work of Christ in the parish. Others may need to look beyond their own parish, perhaps even to what neighboring parishes are doing in certain fields, or their (arch)diocese. One may need to look outside church structures to find appropriate apprenticeship activities.

Throughout this book, the term "apprentice" is used to refer to those being catechized. The term serves as a reminder that those whose formation we have responsibility for are not simply receptacles for catechetical information. They are actively learning how to live as Christians by practicing the Catholic way of life.

Christian Formation for the Entire Parish

Those ministering to catechumens and baptized, uncatechized candidates in the parish initiation process will find this book helpful. It can also be helpful for those ministering to young people in Catholic schools, religious education programs, confirmation preparation programs, and youth ministry programs. For far too long, hours spent doing "service projects" have been required for some sacramental preparation programs. Without a guided reflection upon these kinds of activities, a reflection that puts the activity in conversation with Catholic teaching, those projects can become simply an obstacle to be overcome on the way to a sacrament. The method presented in this book provides that necessary reflection.

This book is also a helpful tool for those working in the area of whole community catechesis. An intergenerational gathering of parishioners could come together to engage in an apprenticeship activity. Age-appropriate catechesis could then break open the experience and pertinent biblical and doctrinal catechesis could be shared. Becoming more committed disciples of Christ need not be solely an intellectual enterprise. Actually doing Christ's work and then reflecting upon it will take root and flourish.

It should be noted that this book was designed first of all for use with adult catechumens and candidates as part of their process of formation for Christian initiation. Thus some of the suggested activities may be less helpful or appropriate for younger apprentices. Catechists are encouraged to use

this book as inspiration for formation of whatever age group they work with, and should feel free to adapt the activities in ways that will best suit their own groups. The important thing is to maintain the method that should always involve the sequence of Word→Apprenticeship Activity→ Mystagogical Catechesis.

Learning "In the Hole"

My youngest brother, Jim, when he was nearing the end of his high school years, decided that he wanted to become an electrician. He was hired by an electrical contractor and worked many hours per week, at minimum wage, for the contractor. Jim enrolled in classes that met every other Thursday night to get "book knowledge" about electrical work. One summer while visiting my family in New England, I was awakened by the early morning rustlings of Jim, who was preparing his lunch for his work day. It was about five o'clock in the morning. Jim returned home from work at about seven that evening, completely covered with dirt and sweat. I gaped at him and asked him how he had spent his day. He said to me, "In a hole. You see, the contractor I work for has the contract for a large doughnut shop chain in southern New England. Today we spent the day installing a drive-through kiosk at one of these shops. We dug a huge hole between the shop and the place where people would order their doughnuts and coffee for pickup at the take-out window. I spent the day in blistering heat, in the hole, with my boss showing me how to make the proper connections." Six months later I received a phone call from Jim, who was bursting with the proud news that he had just received his license in the mail. He was now a licensed electrician in the Commonwealth of Massachusetts.

I share this story because it has so much to do with the way we form people in the Christian way of life. My question: Where did my brother Jim become an electrician? The answer: In the hole! And he also needed every other Thursday night at class to put his practical experience into a kind of conversation with what he was learning in the books. Christian formation is not unlike this experience. Your parish is a hole—a hole in which people seeking to become Christ for others learn how to do that precisely by doing that. Yes, they do need the book knowledge as well. This knowledge must be placed in a conversation with their real work of becoming Christ for the world. I hope this book helps you connect those in Christian formation with what is happening in the hole, what is happening in your parish. After all, what we are about is making disciples committed to bringing the Good News to a world hungry for that news.

Jerry Galipeau, D. Min.

A CATECHETICAL METHOD:

Mystagogical Catechesis in the Session for Christian Formation

After the apprenticeship experience, the leader may wish to employ the following method to initiate a dialogue that addresses the scripture, the apprenticeship experience that flowed out of the scripture, and related Church teaching. This approach begins with the leader facilitating a process that helps break the experience open for the participants. This kind of reflection is "mystagogical" because it attempts to probe the meaning of the experience. Then the applicable Church teaching may be explored more fruitfully.

A. Initial Reflection

If some time has elapsed since the apprenticeship experience, the leader may begin the reflection by helping the participants recall the event and what they did. A simple walk-through of what happened will usually suffice. Begin by reading the scripture text that inspired the apprenticeship activity.

Once the scripture is read and the event has been recalled, it is important that the participants first reflect on the apprenticeship activity at the level of their initial observances and reactions. The purpose of this is to get a clear picture of what took place and their reaction to it so that their later, deeper reflection will be more fruitful. The following questions may be helpful.

1. How were you feeling as you prepared for the activity?
2. Describe the location of the activity. What struck you about the location? Who was present? Does anything or anyone stand out in your mind?
3. What touched you about the experience? Were there any surprises?

B. Deeper Reflection

This next level of reflection probes the experience more deeply, with an eye toward uncovering the meaning of the experience. The leader encourages the participants to make connections between what occurred and the issues of faith and theology that have been emerging in their Christian formation. The following questions may be helpful.

1. Did you sense the presence of God at any time during the event? In what ways?
2. Was your own faith nourished at any time during the activity? Can you name ways that your faith was nourished?
3. Was your understanding of the Church as the Body of Christ expanded in some way?
4. Can you describe a way that you experienced the presence of Christ in those around you during the activity?
5. What did you learn about yourself? What did you learn about the other people who were present?

C. Sharing Church Teaching

After the participants' various reflections, the leader then begins to catechize by placing related Church teaching in dialogue with the experience. This may take the form of a presentation on the related topic. The leader should make it clear that the participants ought to feel free to ask clarifying questions during the presentation. The leader will need to make concrete connections between what is being presented and the reflections of the participants. This is critical to this type of catechesis. The leader will usually find that catechizing a group of persons who have shared a common experience related to the topic will bring much more life to the particular teaching than would be possible otherwise.

D. Conclusion

Once the Church teaching has been shared, the leader may wish to proclaim the original scripture reading again, calling for a moment of silent reflection. The leader may ask the participants to recall ways that they have been formed more and more into the image of Christ through the apprenticeship activity, the reflection, and the teaching. A moment of grateful silence is appropriate. The following questions may be helpful.

1. What have I learned through this experience?
2. In what ways have I experienced change?
3. Can I identify a new direction that God may be calling me to embrace?

E. Closing Prayer

Depending on the makeup of the group, the leader may choose to end the session with one of the blessings or exorcism prayers from the *Rite of Christian Initiation of Adults*. At other times, a priest or deacon might be invited to anoint any catechumens present with the oil of catechumens. A simple prayer of thanksgiving for the experience and the reflection upon that experience would also be most appropriate.

LITURGICAL YEAR A

ADVENT/CHRISTMAS

FIRST SUNDAY OF ADVENT

Isaiah 2:1–5

They shall beat their swords into plowshares . . .
one nation shall not raise the sword against another,
nor shall they train for war again.

Apprenticeship Activity

Does the parish have a peace and justice committee? Are there parishioners who organize letter-writing campaigns to politicians on behalf of those who seek justice and peace throughout the world? Get the apprentices involved in the justice and peace work of the parish.

Christian Formation

Catholic social teaching on peace and justice

◆

Catechetical Resources

U.S. Bishops: *The Challenge of Peace: God's Promise and Our Response, A Pastoral Letter on War and Peace* §27–29, 326–329
Pope John XXIII: *Pacem in Terris* §35–36, 166–172
Catechism of the Catholic Church (CCC) §1928–1948, 2302–2317
United States Catholic Catechism for Adults (USCCA) pp. 420–425

SECOND SUNDAY OF ADVENT

Romans 15:4–9

Welcome one another, then, as Christ welcomed you,
for the glory of God.

Apprenticeship Activity

Does the parish have an organized ministry of hospitality and welcome? How can we help connect the apprentices with the hospitality ministry of the parish? If people are stationed at the entrances of the parish church to welcome worshipers, why not pair them with an apprentice before one of the Sunday Masses?

Christian Formation

Aim and purpose of the introductory rites for Mass

Catechetical Resources

General Instruction of the Roman Missal §27 and The Introductory Rites, §46–54
USCCA p. 218

THIRD SUNDAY OF ADVENT

Psalm 146: 6–7, 8–9, 9–10
The LORD God keeps faith forever,
secures justice for the oppressed,
gives food to the hungry.
The LORD sets captives free.

Apprenticeship Activity

Does the parish support its own or a local food pantry? Does the parish assist in the distribution of meals to the hungry? Schedule a time when the apprentices can be connected with this ministry.

Christian Formation

Church's solidarity with the poor

◆

Catechetical Resources

U.S. Bishops: Pastoral Letter *Economic Justice for All*
Pope Leo XIII: *The Condition of Labor,* Rerum Novarum §24, 28–30
Pope Paul VI: *The Development of Peoples,* Populorum Progressio §43, 44, 51, 57, 61, 73, 76
CCC §1939–1942, 2443–2449
USCCA pp. 420–425, 427–428, 454–456

FOURTH SUNDAY OF ADVENT

Matthew 1:18–24
This is how the birth of Jesus Christ came about.
When his mother Mary was betrothed to Joseph, but before
they lived together, she was found with child
through the Holy Spirit.

Apprenticeship Activity

Does the parish have an outreach to those in crisis pregnancies? Is there a local agency that assists young needy mothers in caring for their children? Are there families in the parish who have supported one of their children through an unplanned pregnancy? Consider inviting people who assist young women through these pregnancies to speak at a session. Are there some apprentices who are "naturals" in this important work?

Christian Formation

Dignity of the human person, solidarity with those in crisis

Catechetical Resources

CCC §1939–1948, 2222–2233
USCCA pp. 387–390, 456

CHRISTMAS

Luke 2:1–14

She wrapped him in swaddling clothes
and laid him in a manger,
because there was no room for them in the inn.

Christian Formation

Church's commitment to care
for the poor

◆

Catechetical Resources

U.S. Bishops: Pastoral Letter *Economic Justice for All* §28–30
Pope Leo XIII: *The Condition of Labor, Rerum Novarum*
Pope John XXIII: *On Christianity and Social Progress*, Mater et Magistra §159–160
Pope Paul VI: *The Development of Peoples*, Populorum Progressio §43, 44, 51, 57, 61, 73, 76
John Paul II: *On Social Concern*, Sollicitudo Rei Socialis §17, 41–45
CCC §2443–2449
USCCA pp. 420–425, 427–428, 454–456

Apprenticeship Activity

Does the parish have an active outreach program to assist the homeless? Does the parish Saint Vincent de Paul Society or other organization assist those who have difficulty paying their utility bills? Invite the apprentices to become involved in this critical ministry.

THE HOLY FAMILY
OF JESUS, MARY, AND JOSEPH

Sirach 3:2–7, 12–14

My son, take care of your father when he is old;
. . . Even if his mind fail, be considerate of him.

Christian Formation

Dignity of the human person,
especially the elderly

◆

Catechetical Resources

Pope John Paul II: *The Gospel of Life*, Evangelium Vitae §15, 46, 64, 94
USCCA pp. 456, 337, 377–378

Apprenticeship Activity

Does the parish have a ministry of care for the aging? Are there regular visits to local nursing homes and long-term care facilities? Connect apprentices with those who minister to the aging for a pastoral visit.

THE SOLEMNITY OF THE BLESSED VIRGIN MARY, THE MOTHER OF GOD

Luke 2:16–21
The shepherds went in haste to Bethlehem and found Mary and Joseph, and the infant lying in the manger.

Apprenticeship Activity

Does the parish have a group of parishioners who regularly pray the rosary or engage in another type of Marian devotion? Is it possible to invite them to a session to share their faith and Marian devotional life with the apprentices? This could be an opportunity for these people to teach the apprentices the rosary and other Marian devotional prayers.

Christian Formation

Marian devotion

◆

Catechetical Resources

CCC §971–975
USCCA pp. 298–301, 538–539

THE EPIPHANY OF THE LORD

Ephesians 3:2–3a, 5–6
. . . it has now been revealed . . . that the Gentiles are coheirs, members of the same body, and copartners in the promise in Christ Jesus through the gospel.

Christian Formation

Christian unity

◆

Catechetical Resources

Second Vatican Council:
   Decree on Ecumenism §1–12
CCC §820
USCCA p. 128

Apprenticeship Activity

How will the parish mark the Week of Christian Unity? Does the parish partner with other Christian denominations in social justice or service projects? Connect apprentices with these efforts.

THE BAPTISM OF THE LORD

Acts 10:34–38

. . . God anointed Jesus of Nazareth with the Holy Spirit and power. He went about doing good and healing all those oppressed by the devil, for God was with him.

Apprenticeship Activity

Does the parish invite confirmation candidates to become a part of the parish's service and outreach to the needy? If this kind of program is in place, consider inviting the apprentices to accompany these confirmation candidates on one of their service projects.

Christian Formation

Church's ministry to the poor

◆

Catechetical Resources

U.S. Bishops: Pastoral Letter *Economic Justice for All* §174–178, 181, 182, 185, 188, 192, 215

Pope Leo XIII: *The Condition of Labor*, Rerum Novarum §28, 29

Pope John XXIII: *On Christianity and Social Progress*, Mater et Magistra §159–160

Pope Paul VI: *The Development of Peoples*, Populorum Progressio §43, 44, 51, 57, 61, 73, 76

John Paul II: *On Social Concern*, Sollicitudo Rei Socialis §17, 41–45

CCC §1939–1948, 2443–2449

USCCA pp. 420–425, 427–428, 454–456

LENT

During Lent, if a parish has two "tracks," one for the elect and another for catechumens and candidates who will not celebrate the sacraments until the following year, the following ideas may be used with those bypassing the sacraments. The elect will be on their own journey, preparing for, celebrating, and reflecting upon the celebration of the scrutinies.

FIRST SUNDAY OF LENT

Psalm 51: 3–4, 5–6, 12–13, 17
For I acknowledge my offense,
and my sin is before me always.

Apprenticeship Activity

Is the parish planning a communal celebration of the rite of reconciliation or a non-sacramental penitential service? Lent is the opportune time to focus the attention of apprentices on the Church's ministry of reconciliation. Invite those in the initiation process to the celebration.

Christian Formation

Church as the sacrament of reconciliation

◆

Catechetical Resources

CCC §1422–1460
USCCA pp. 233–247

SECOND SUNDAY OF LENT

Matthew 17:1–9
And he was transfigured before them.

Apprenticeship Activity

Is there someone who has gone through the initiation process in the past who was "transfigured" before your eyes? Is there someone who can witness to the tremendous power of the reconciling love of God, someone whose life made a dramatic turn? Invite that person to share his or her story of conversion.

Christian Formation

Conversion and reconciliation

◆

Catechetical Resources

Rite of Penance, Introduction
CCC §1422–1460, 1848–1876
USCCA pp. 236–237

THIRD SUNDAY OF LENT

John 4:5–42

*"The water I shall give will become in him a spring of water
welling up to eternal life."*

Apprenticeship Activity

Does the parish have a baptism preparation program
for parents of infants? If a preparation session is
scheduled during Lent, invite the apprentices to
attend. Their appreciation for their own baptism or
preparation for that sacrament at a later time will be
greatly enhanced.

Christian Formation

Sacrament of baptism

◆

Catechetical Resources

*Rite of Christian Initiation of
Adults (RCIA)* or
Sacramentary, Blessing of
Water for the Easter Vigil
RCIA, Introduction
Rite of Baptism for Children,
Introduction
CCC §1213–1284
USCCA pp. 181–199

FOURTH SUNDAY OF LENT

John 9:1–41

*"The man called Jesus made clay and anointed my eyes
and told me, 'Go to Siloam and wash.' So I went there
and washed and was able to see."*

Apprenticeship Activity

Does the parish have a team that visits local hospitals to
call on those who are sick or to bring the Eucharist to
Catholic patients? Consider inviting the apprentices to
go along with some of these ministers as they perform a
central healing ministry of the Church.

Christian Formation

Church's ministry of healing

◆

Catechetical Resources

*Rite of Anointing and Pastoral Care of
the Sick*, Introduction
CCC §1499–1532
USCCA pp. 251–259

FIFTH SUNDAY OF LENT

Ezekiel 37:12–14

O my people, I will open your graves and have you rise from them.

Apprenticeship Activity

In order to underscore the Church's teaching proclaiming the resurrection of the dead at the end of time, consider visiting a local cemetery. There you will find headstones and inscriptions that are wonderful catechetical tools to help discover the faith of believers, even in the face of death. This may also be an opportunity to ask a priest or deacon who conducts graveside services to explain the symbols and words of that important step in the Church's Order of Christian Funerals.

Christian Formation

Funerals, Christian death, resurrection of the body

◆

Catechetical Resources

Order of Christian Funerals,
  Introduction
CCC §1680–1690
USCCA pp. 153–162

PALM SUNDAY OF THE LORD'S PASSION

Matthew 26:14 – 27:66

But Jesus cried out again in a loud voice, and gave up his spirit.

Christian Formation

Stations of the Cross, paschal mystery

◆

Apprenticeship Activity

If the parish celebrates the Stations of the Cross, invite the apprentices to take part in this devotional practice.

Catechetical Resources

Rite of Penance, Introduction
CCC §571–637
USCCA pp. 91–93

EASTER TRIDUUM

There is no better way to form people in the Catholic faith than to walk with them through the celebration of the Triduum. Invite them to take part in the washing of feet on Holy Thursday, the veneration of the cross on Good Friday, and the celebration of the initiation sacraments at the Easter Vigil. Invite the apprentices to make this three-day festival a retreat experience.

SECOND SUNDAY OF EASTER

John 20:19–31
Jesus came and stood in their midst and said to them,
"Peace be with you."

Apprenticeship Activity

Peace is a sure sign of the presence of the risen Christ. Are there people in the parish who are part of a group that works locally and globally for peace? Invite the apprentices to attend one of their meetings, or have these people attend a session with the apprentices in order to share their convictions and passion for peace.

Christian Formation

Catholic social teaching on peace and justice

◆

Catechetical Resources
U.S. Bishops: *The Challenge of Peace: God's Promise and Our Response, A Pastoral Letter on War and Peace* §27–29, 52–54
Pope John XXIII: *Pacem in Terris* §35, 36, 166–172
CCC §1928–1948, 2302–2317
USCCA pp. 332–333

THIRD SUNDAY OF EASTER

Luke 24:13–35

*"Were not our hearts burning within us while he spoke to us
on the way and opened the Scriptures to us?"*

Apprenticeship Activity

Do the priests and deacons responsible for preaching meet each week with a group of parishioners who assist them in preparing their homilies? If so, invite the apprentices to take part in one of these sessions. If not, suggest this practice to your priests and deacons and take the responsibility to craft a preparation session.

Christian Formation

Preaching the gospel of Christ

◆

Catechetical Resources

U.S. Bishops: *Fulfilled in Your Hearing: The Homily in the Sunday Assembly*
Lectionary for Mass, Introduction
USCCA pp. 24–26, 171–172

FOURTH SUNDAY OF EASTER

John 10:1–10

"The sheep follow him, because they recognize his voice."

Apprenticeship Activity

If you live in or near a place that raises sheep, arrange a field trip. Even a trip to a local zoo to observe sheep is a good idea. The images of Christ as the Good Shepherd and us as the sheep of his flock really hit home when one observes sheep even for a short period of time!

Christian Formation

Christ is the Good Shepherd

◆

Catechetical Resources

Vatican Council II: *Dogmatic Constitution on the Church*, Lumen Gentium §6–8, 18
USCCA pp. 258–259

FIFTH SUNDAY OF EASTER

Acts 6:1–7

*They presented these men to the apostles who prayed
and laid hands on them.*

Apprenticeship Activity

Spring is the usual time of year when dioceses ordain priests and deacons. Call your diocesan chancery office or pastoral center to find out when an ordination is scheduled. Bring the apprentices to the ordination.

Christian Formation

Sacrament of holy orders

◆

Catechetical Resources

Rites of Ordination, Introduction
CCC §1533–1600
USCCA pp. 261–275

SIXTH SUNDAY OF EASTER

1 Peter 3:15–18

*Always be ready to give an explanation to anyone who asks you
for a reason for your hope.*

Apprenticeship Activity

Do you know of a parishioner who is ill, but remains an ambassador of hope because of his or her faith? Invite that person to the session to share their story of hope in the face of great pain.

Christian Formation

The Christian virtue of hope

◆

Catechetical Resources

CCC §2090–2092
USCCA pp. 317, 333, 534

THE ASCENSION OF THE LORD

Psalm 47: 2–3, 6–7, 8–9
Sing praise to God, sing praise.

Apprenticeship Activity

Catholics sing and make music in praise of God. Invite the apprentices to attend part or all of a choir rehearsal. If this is not convenient, invite members of the parish's music ministry to your session with the apprentices. Invite them to witness to the power of music in their faith lives. Be sure to include singing throughout the session!

Christian Formation

Music in Catholic worship

◆

Catechetical Resources

U.S. Bishops: *Music in Catholic Worship, Liturgical Music Today*
CCC §1156–1158
USCCA pp. 171, 175

SEVENTH SUNDAY OF EASTER

Acts 1:12–14
All these devoted themselves with one accord to prayer,
together with some women, and Mary the mother of Jesus,
and his brothers.

Apprenticeship Activity

Does the parish have a women's club or Ladies' Sodality? Women play vital roles in parish life. Invite the apprentices to attend part or all of a meeting of these women's groups. You may want to invite a group of women who represent the various ministries of the parish to attend a session.

Christian Formation

The role of women in the Church

◆

Catechetical Resources

Holy See: *Letter to the Bishops of the Catholic Church on the Collaboration of Men and Women in the Church and in the World* §8, 13–17
John Paul II: *The Genius of Women*
USCCA pp. 134–135

PENTECOST

John 20:19–23
"Receive the Holy Spirit."

Apprenticeship Activity

Many parishes celebrate the sacrament of confirmation with young people during the Easter season. Invite the apprentices to attend this celebration. Or you may want to invite the confirmation catechists to a session with the apprentices to share their experiences of preparing young people for this sacrament of initiation.

Christian Formation

Sacrament of confirmation

◆

Catechetical Resources

Rite of Confirmation, Introduction
CCC §1285–1321
USCCA pp. 102–110, 201–211

ORDINARY TIME

THE SOLEMNITY OF THE MOST HOLY TRINITY

2 Corinthians 13:11–13

Mend your ways, encourage one another, agree with one another,
live in peace, and the God of love and peace will be with you.

Apprenticeship Activity

The love among the Father, Son, and Holy Spirit creates a bond within the Holy Trinity. This love is what holds Catholic families together as well. Does the parish have a family life ministry? Do they schedule Catholic family events? Invite the apprentices to one of these events or invite the family life leaders to a session with the apprentices.

Christian Formation

The Trinity, Catholic family life

◆

Catechetical Resources

CCC §238–267
USCCA pp. 51–53, 373–385

THE SOLEMNITY OF THE MOST HOLY BODY AND BLOOD OF CHRIST

1 Corinthians 10:16–17

The cup of blessing that we bless,
is it not a participation in the blood of Christ?

Apprenticeship Activity

Today's solemnity is an ideal time to schedule a tour of the sacristy and for the apprentices to meet and speak with the parish sacristans and/or Mass coordinators. Be sure to have the sacristan show the apprentices the various vessels, vestments, and sacramentals used in the Church's liturgical life.

Christian Formation

The liturgy

◆

Catechetical Resources

General Instruction of the
Roman Missal §16
Constitution on the Sacred Liturgy
§1, 2, 7–14
CCC §1066–1075
USCCA pp. 165–179, 213–232

SECOND SUNDAY IN ORDINARY TIME

John 1:29–34

"Behold, the Lamb of God, who takes away the sin of the world."

Apprenticeship Activity

One of the primary means through which the Church affirms the reality that Christ came to take away the sins of the world is the celebration of the sacrament of reconciliation. Is this a good week to visit the parish's reconciliation room? Perhaps apprentices could be invited to listen to a parishioner who celebrates the sacrament regularly.

Christian Formation

Sacrament of reconciliation

◆

Catechetical Resources

Rite of Penance, Introduction
CCC §1422–1460
USCCA pp. 233–247

THIRD SUNDAY IN ORDINARY TIME

Matthew 4:12–23

"Come after me, and I will make you fishers of men."

Apprenticeship Activity

The parish priest is someone who has answered the vocational call to ordained ministry. Invite your priest(s) to a session, not to give a theology of priesthood, but to witness to God's initial and continuing call and how this has been lived out. Perhaps a tour of or an open house at the rectory could be arranged.

Christian Formation

The priesthood

◆

Catechetical Resources

Rites of Ordination, Introduction
CCC §1539–1554
USCCA pp. 261–275

FOURTH SUNDAY IN ORDINARY TIME

Matthew 5:1-12a
"Blessed are they who mourn,
for they will be comforted."

Apprenticeship Activity

Does the parish have a ministry to the bereaved? Consider inviting one or two apprentices to attend a meeting of the bereavement ministry, being sure to let the leaders and participants know that these are people being formed in the Catholic way of life. If this is not possible, invite the bereavement ministers to share their own stories with the apprentices.

Christian Formation

Grief and bereavement

◆

Catechetical Resources

Order of Christian Funerals,
Introduction
USCCA pp. 252–253

FIFTH SUNDAY IN ORDINARY TIME

Isaiah 58:7–10
Share your bread with the hungry,
shelter the oppressed and the homeless.

Apprenticeship Activity

Does the parish have a St. Vincent de Paul Society? If there are no organized attempts in the parish to feed the poor and shelter the homeless, find organizations in your local community. Arrange to have the apprentices take part in serving a meal to the hungry or arranging for shelter for those with no home.

Christian Formation

Church's solidarity with the poor

◆

Catechetical Resources

Catholic Relief Services Web site materials
U.S. Bishops: Pastoral Letter *Economic Justice for All* §174–178, 181, 182, 185, 188, 192, 215
Pope Leo XIII: *The Condition of Labor,* Rerum Novarum §28–30
Pope John XXIII: *On Christianity and Social Progress,* Mater et Magistra §159–160
Pope Paul VI: *The Development of Peoples,* Populorum Progressio §43, 44, 51, 57, 61, 73, 76
John Paul II: *On Social Concern,* Sollicitudo Rei Socialis §17, 41–45
CCC §1939–1942, 2443–2449
USCCA pp. 420–425, 427–428, 454–456

SIXTH SUNDAY IN ORDINARY TIME

Matthew 5:17–37

"And if your right hand causes you to sin, cut it off and throw it away."

Apprenticeship Activity

Do you know of someone in the parish or perhaps on the initiation team who has a deep story of conversion that can be shared with the apprentices? Since the initiation process is centered on conversion, today is a perfect time for all to hear a story of real conversion, when a person sacrificed a great deal to say "yes" to God and "no" to sinful behavior. Use this story as a launching point for a "sponsor walk," in which the apprentices are asked to share stories about their own journeys of conversion.

Christian Formation

Conversion and reconciliation

◆

Catechetical Resources

Rite of Penance, Introduction
CCC §1422–1460, 1848–1876
USCCA pp. 236–237

SEVENTH SUNDAY IN ORDINARY TIME

Matthew 5:38–48

"But I say to you, love your enemies and pray for those who persecute you."

Christian Formation

Forgiveness of enemies

◆

Catechetical Resources

Rite of Penance: Introduction
U.S. Bishops: *The Challenge of Peace: God's Promise and Our Response, A Pastoral Letter on War and Peace* §46, 52–54, 290, 300
Pope John XXIII: *Pacem in Terris* §35–36, 166–172
CCC § 1928–1948, 2302–2317
USCCA pp. 488, 494

Apprenticeship Activity

This is one of the most difficult of the Lord's sayings for the believer to grasp. Arrange a simple prayer service to pray specifically for enemies, those against whom we hold grudges, those in the workplace or in families who "persecute us."

EIGHTH SUNDAY IN ORDINARY TIME

Matthew 6:24–34
"Why are you anxious about clothes?"

Apprenticeship Activity

Have someone (an apprentice, a sponsor, or a member of the team) volunteer for a "closet visit." Set the ground rules in advance. Let everyone know that the person has volunteered to sift through all their clothing in order to give to the poor anything that has not been worn in one year. Everyone accompanies the volunteer to his or her home and to the clothes closet. This can be a humorous activity, but one that is a great challenge to those being configured to Christ. The principle here is "Live simply so that others may simply live."

Christian Formation

Stewardship

◆

Catechetical Resources

U.S. Bishops: *Our Hearts Were Burning Within Us: A Pastoral Plan for Adult Faith Formation in the United States* §71, 122

The International Catholic Stewardship Council has excellent resources on its Web site: www.catholicstewardship.org

USCCA pp. 450–455

NINTH SUNDAY IN ORDINARY TIME

Matthew 7:21–27
"Everyone who listens to these words of mine and acts on them will be like a wise man who built his house on rock."

Apprenticeship Activity

The catechumenate process is one piece of the catechetical and formational ministries of the parish. Invite small groups of apprentices to a religious formation class for the children of the parish. This important area of ministry is at the heart of parish life, but often goes largely unnoticed. Who knows, the apprentices might see catechesis as a future ministry for them as initiated Catholics!

Christian Formation

The catechetical ministry of the Church: Sharing the tradition

◆

Catechetical Resources

U.S. Bishops: *Our Hearts Were Burning Within Us: A Pastoral Plan for Adult Faith Formation in the United States* §38–44, 84–96

Holy See: *General Directory for Catechesis*, Chapter 1

TENTH SUNDAY IN ORDINARY TIME

Matthew 9:9–13
"I did not come to call the righteous but sinners."

Apprenticeship Activity

Today provides a perfect opportunity for some good "conversion therapy." Apprentices can forget that they are sinners like the rest of us. Ask them, as well as everyone on the initiation team, to spend time in quiet reflection, focusing on this line from Matthew's Gospel. Ask them to write down how they are learning to turn away from sin. You may want to ask them to talk about this with their sponsors. You could conclude this event with a penitential service asking for God's forgiveness and praising God for boundless mercy.

Christian Formation

Conversion and reconciliation

◆

Catechetical Resources

Rite of Penance, Introduction
CCC §1422–1460, 1848–1876
USCCA pp. 236–237

ELEVENTH SUNDAY IN ORDINARY TIME

Matthew 9:36 – 10:8
"Then he summoned his twelve disciples and
gave them authority over unclean spirits to drive them out and to cure
every disease and every illness."

Apprenticeship Activity

Is there a Catholic hospital or Catholic health care system in your area? Contact the person in charge of implementing the mission and vision of Catholic health care and arrange a visit to the hospital for an explanation of this vision, a vital ministry of the Church.

Christian Formation

Catholic health care

◆

Catechetical Resources

Various materials on Catholic health care from the Catholic Health Association at www.chausa.org

TWELFTH SUNDAY IN ORDINARY TIME

Matthew 10:26–33

*"So do not be afraid . . . Everyone who acknowledges me before others I will
acknowledge before my heavenly Father."*

Apprenticeship Activity

Invite the apprentices to think of one person they
spend time with (at work, school, among their
friends), whom they see on a fairly regular basis, who
is not aware that they are on this faith journey. Ask
them to consider discussing what's been happening in
their lives with this person some time in the coming
week. Spend time at the next session discussing
reactions.

Christian Formation

Evangelization

◆

Catechetical Resources

Pope Paul VI: *Evangelii Nuntiandi*
Pope John Paul II: *The New
Evangelization*
U.S. Bishops: *Our Hearts Were Burning
Within Us: A Pastoral Plan for Adult
Faith Formation in the United States*
USCCA pp. 16–17, 134–136, 502

THIRTEENTH SUNDAY IN ORDINARY TIME

Matthew 10:37–42

*"Whoever does not take up his cross
and follow after me is not worthy of me."*

Apprenticeship Activity

Have someone from the parish who has been given a
great cross to bear and bears that cross with faith and
hope share his or her story with the group. Invite the
apprentices to react to this person's story. You may
want to invite them to relate to their sponsor, or to
the group, the cross that they bear. The session could
conclude with a simple veneration of the cross.

Christian Formation

The cross, paschal mystery

◆

Catechetical Resources

The Creed
CCC §571–637
USCCA pp. 91–93, 165–179

FOURTEENTH SUNDAY IN ORDINARY TIME

Matthew 11:25–30

"Come to me, all you who labor and are burdened, and I will give you rest."

Apprenticeship Activity

Does your parish have an outreach ministry to those who have come to the end of their lives? Is it possible to arrange visits, with ministers of care, to those who are confined to their homes or care centers? Do you have parishioners who are connected with hospice programs? Invite them to share their experiences with the group.

Christian Formation

Christian death

◆

Catechetical Resources

Order of Christian Funerals,
   Introduction
CCC §1020–1060
USCCA pp. 158–159

FIFTEENTH SUNDAY IN ORDINARY TIME

Matthew 13:1–23

*"But the seed sown on rich soil is the one
who hears the word and understands it."*

Christian Formation

Preaching the gospel of Christ

◆

Apprenticeship Activity

Priests and deacons are entrusted with the ministry of preaching each Sunday. If the priest or deacon meets with a group of parishioners to prepare the homily, why not ask if the apprentices can join the group? If there are no such planning meetings, ask the priest or deacon to arrange a special meeting with the apprentices to assist him in preparing his homily.

Catechetical Resources

U.S. Bishops: *Fulfilled in Your Hearing:
   The Homily in the Sunday Assembly*
Lectionary for Mass, Introduction
USCCA pp. 24–26, 171–172

SIXTEENTH SUNDAY IN ORDINARY TIME

Romans 8:26–27

The Spirit comes to the aid of our weakness; for we do not know how to pray as we ought.

Apprenticeship Activity

Does the parish have organized prayer services during the week, such as morning or evening prayer? If so, invite the apprentices to the prayer service, being sure to lead them in a reflection upon the ritual following the prayer service. If the parish does not have organized prayer services, consider preparing and praying vespers, including the lighting of incense and the praying of Psalm 141.

Christian Formation

Prayer

◆

Catechetical Resources

Liturgy of the Hours, Introduction
CCC §2558ff
USCCA pp. 461–495

SEVENTEENTH SUNDAY IN ORDINARY TIME

Matthew 13:44–52

*"The kingdom of heaven is like a treasure buried in a field . . .
a merchant searching for fine pearls . . . a net thrown into the sea."*

Apprenticeship Activity

Christian art has inspired the faith of believers for centuries. Today's Gospel parables show us that the Lord used imagery to lead his followers to belief. Is there a museum in the area that has a collection of Christian art? Consider a field trip, or borrow Christian art books from the library and share these images with the apprentices. Is there an art historian in the parish or at a local college who can speak on the history of Christian art? Does the parish church or another church in the area have stained glass windows that tell some of the stories of salvation or recount the lives of the saints? Make a visit to these windows a field trip!

Christian Formation

Christian art

◆

Catechetical Resources

Books on Christian art, parish stained glass windows, statuary, etc.
CCC §2502–2503
USCCA p. 433

EIGHTEENTH SUNDAY IN ORDINARY TIME

Matthew 14:13–21

"There is no need for them to go away; give them some food yourselves."

Apprenticeship Activity

Is there a parish-sponsored soup kitchen or local outreach to the hungry? Is there a "meals-on-wheels" program in the community? Connect the apprentices with these programs. One night serving a meal in a soup kitchen could be worth more than the finest lecture on Catholic social teaching!

Christian Formation

Church's solidarity with the poor

◆

Catechetical Resources

U.S. Bishops: Pastoral Letter *Economic Justice for All* §174–178, 181, 182, 185, 188, 192, 215

Pope Leo XIII: *The Condition of Labor*, Rerum Novarum §28, 29

Pope Paul VI: *The Development of Peoples*, Populorum Progressio §43, 44, 51, 57, 61, 73, 76

John Paul II: *On Social Concern*, Sollicitudo Rei Socialis §17, 41–45

CCC §1939–1942, 2443–2449

USCCA pp. 420–425, 427–428, 454–456

NINETEENTH SUNDAY IN ORDINARY TIME

Matthew 14:22–33

He went up on the mountain by himself to pray.

Apprenticeship Activity

Many initiation programs spend too much time in the giving of information, either orally or through handouts, videos, and other media. Consider providing the opportunity for the apprentices to spend a significant period of time in solitary prayer.

Christian Formation

Prayer

◆

Catechetical Resources

CCC §2558ff

USCCA pp. 461–495

TWENTIETH SUNDAY IN ORDINARY TIME

Isaiah 56:1, 6–7
*For my house shall be called
a house of prayer for all peoples.*

Apprenticeship Activity

Is there a gathering of local pastors or parishioners who have formed an ecumenical group? Consider inviting the apprentices to sit in on one of these meetings.

Christian Formation

Ecumenism

◆

Catechetical Resources

Second Vatican Council:
  Decree on Ecumenism
CCC §820
USCCA p. 128

TWENTY-FIRST SUNDAY IN ORDINARY TIME

Matthew 16:13–20
*"And so I say to you, you are Peter, and upon this rock
I will build my church."*

Apprenticeship Activity

Your bishop (the ordinary of the diocese or an auxiliary) has a key role to play in the formation of Catholics in your diocese or archdiocese. Consider inviting the bishop to one of your formation sessions. Be sure to contact him well in advance in order to be placed on his schedule. This might also be a good opportunity to set up a tour of your diocesan offices.

Christian Formation

The ministry of the bishop

◆

Catechetical Resources

CCC §1554–1561
USCCA pp. 265–266

TWENTY-SECOND SUNDAY IN ORDINARY TIME

Matthew 16:21–27
"Whoever wishes to come after me must deny himself,
take up his cross, and follow me."

Apprenticeship Activity

There are many places in your community where Christians carry the cross every day of their lives. Consider organizing a visit to the cancer unit of a local children's hospital. Is there someone in the parish who carries a particularly heavy cross and whose faith shines through? Consider inviting that person to speak with the apprentices.

Christian Formation

The cross, paschal mystery

◆

Catechetical Resources

The Creed
CCC §571–637
USCCA pp. 91–93, 165–179

TWENTY-THIRD SUNDAY IN ORDINARY TIME

Romans 13:8–10
"You shall love your neighbor as yourself."

Apprenticeship Activity

A great outreach ministry that shares the love of the parish community occurs when a parishioner brings Communion to someone who is homebound. Consider pairing the apprentices with some of these ministers as they bring Communion to the sick and confined.

Christian Formation

Extraordinary ministry of the Eucharist, ministry of care

◆

Catechetical Resources

Rite of Anointing and Pastoral Care of the Sick, Introduction
The list of spiritual and corporal works of mercy
CCC §1500–1510, 2447–2448
USCCA pp. 225–227, 254

TWENTY-FOURTH SUNDAY IN ORDINARY TIME

Matthew 18:21–35

"Lord, if my brother sins against me, how often must I forgive? As many as seven times?"
Jesus answered, "I say to you, not seven times but seventy-seven times."

Apprenticeship Activity

In a focus on the ministry of healing and reconciliation, consider arranging a tour of the parish reconciliation room. Perhaps a priest could explain the church's many ministries of healing and walk the apprentices through the celebration of the sacraments of reconciliation and anointing of the sick.

Christian Formation

Forgiveness and the sacrament of reconciliation

◆

Catechetical Resources

Rite of Penance, Introduction
CCC §1422–1460
USCCA pp. 234–247

TWENTY-FIFTH SUNDAY IN ORDINARY TIME

Psalm 145:2–3, 8–9, 17–18

Every day will I bless you,
and I will praise your name forever and ever.

Apprenticeship Activity

Does the parish celebrate Mass on a daily basis? If so, invite some members of the "daily Mass community" to a session with the apprentices. Ask these daily communicants to share their stories of faith and how their daily celebration of the Eucharist sustains them on their spiritual journeys.

Christian Formation

The Mass in the life of the Catholic

◆

Catechetical Resources

CCC §1345–1419
USCCA pp. 213–232

TWENTY-SIXTH SUNDAY IN ORDINARY TIME

Philippians 2:1–11
Do nothing out of selfishness or out of vainglory;
rather, humbly regard others as more important than yourselves,
each looking out not for his own interests, but also for those of others.

Apprenticeship Activity

Does the parish have a parish council, finance council, or various commissions that meet on a regular basis? If so, invite apprentices to attend one of these meetings. This may give them an opportunity to witness how parishioners work together to reach consensus on important matters involving the ministries of the parish.

Christian Formation

Organization of the parish

◆

Catechetical Resources

Parish mission statement
Parish description of various
   commissions/committees/ministries
CCC §2179
USCCA pp. 134–135

TWENTY-SEVENTH SUNDAY IN ORDINARY TIME

Philippians 4:6–9
Keep on doing what you have learned and received and heard and seen in me.
Then the God of peace will be with you.

Apprenticeship Activity

Invite a few people who have traveled the journey of conversion through the Rite of Christian Initiation of Adults in the past to attend a session and witness to how they have persevered on their journey. Invite them to share triumphs as well as challenges.

Christian Formation

Conversion and reconciliation

◆

Catechetical Resources

Rite of Penance, Introduction
CCC §1422–1460, 1848–1876
USCCA pp. 236–237

TWENTY-EIGHTH SUNDAY IN ORDINARY TIME

Isaiah 25:6–10a
The Lord GOD will wipe away
the tears from every face.

Apprenticeship Activity

Does the parish have a ministry to the bereaved? Discuss with the leadership of the bereavement team the possibility of a small number of apprentices attending a meeting. Or invite the bereavement team to a session with the apprentices to talk about the ministry. Perhaps they might be willing to suggest a person who has traveled the journey of grief to come and speak to the group.

Christian Formation

Grief and bereavement:
The Catholic perspective

◆

Catechetical Resources

Order of Christian Funerals,
   Introduction
CCC §1023–1060
USCCA pp. 252–253

TWENTY-NINTH SUNDAY IN ORDINARY TIME

Matthew 22:15–21
"Then repay to Caesar what belongs to Caesar
and to God what belongs to God."

Christian Formation

Stewardship

◆

Catechetical Resources

U.S. Bishops: *Our Hearts Were Burning Within Us: A Pastoral Plan for Adult Faith Formation in the United States* §71, 122
National Catholic Development Conference materials found on its Web site: www.ncdcusa.org
The International Catholic Stewardship Council has excellent resources on its Web site: www.catholicstewardship.org
USCCA pp. 450–455

Apprenticeship Activity

Does the parish have an approach to stewardship of time, talent, and treasure? Is there a stewardship committee? Apprentices often ask questions about how much they are expected to give back to God out of their finances. Invite people who practice a stewardship way of life to speak to the group.

THIRTIETH SUNDAY IN ORDINARY TIME

Exodus 22:20–26

You shall not molest or oppress an alien, for you were once aliens yourselves in the land of Egypt.

Apprenticeship Activity

Does the parish provide a special welcome to those who join the parish? Is there an organized welcoming committee? If they sponsor a social event, be sure to invite the apprentices. Have a member of the welcoming committee or someone on the parish staff describe what a Catholic needs to do in order to join a new parish. This information might come in handy in the future if the family relocates.

Christian Formation

The virtue of Christian hospitality

◆

Catechetical Resources

General Instruction on the Roman Missal, Introductory Rites of Mass

---

THIRTY-FIRST SUNDAY IN ORDINARY TIME

Psalm 131:1, 2, 3

In you, Lord, I have found my peace . . .
I have stilled and quieted
my soul like a weaned child.

Christian Formation

Prayer

◆

Apprenticeship Activity

Does the parish have an organized prayer group? Are there small Christian communities that meet on a regular basis for prayer and reflection? Arrange for the apprentices to visit a prayer group or a small Christian community.

Catechetical Resources

Liturgy of the Hours, Introduction
CCC §2558ff
USCCA pp. 461–495

THIRTY-SECOND SUNDAY IN ORDINARY TIME

Psalm 63:2, 3–4, 5–6, 7–8
Thus have I gazed toward you in the sanctuary
to see your power and your glory.

Apprenticeship Activity

Does the parish regularly schedule adoration of the Blessed Sacrament, or does the parish or a nearby parish have perpetual Eucharistic adoration? Invite the apprentices to adoration at one of these places. Perhaps someone who spends extended periods of time before the Blessed Sacrament could share his or her faith with the group.

Christian Formation

Adoration of the Blessed Sacrament

◆

Catechetical Resources

Order for the Solemn Exposition of the Holy Eucharist, Introduction
CCC §1378–1381
USCCA pp. 223–224, 226–228, 364–365

THIRTY-THIRD SUNDAY IN ORDINARY TIME

Proverbs 31:10–13, 19–20, 30–31
When one finds a worthy wife,
her value is far beyond pearls.

Christian Formation

Christian marriage

◆

Catechetical Resources

Rite of Marriage, Introduction
CCC §1601–1666
USCCA pp. 277–292

Apprenticeship Activity

Does the parish have a marriage preparation program? Is there a pre-Cana program in the area? If so, invite those who minister in these programs to a session with the apprentices. Ask them to explain the process as well as witness to God's presence and action in their own marriages.

THIRTY-FOURTH OR LAST SUNDAY IN ORDINARY TIME
THE SOLEMNITY OF OUR LORD JESUS CHRIST THE KING

Matthew 25:31–46
"I was hungry and you gave me food, I was thirsty and you gave me drink,
a stranger and you welcomed me, naked and you clothed me,
ill and you cared for me, in prison and you visited me."

Apprenticeship Activity

This important passage from Matthew's Gospel provides a blueprint for how Christians are to live. Arrange for the apprentices to be involved in any outreach to the poor during Thanksgiving. If food baskets are prepared and delivered, make sure the apprentices are on the "front lines" of this important ministry.

Christian Formation

Church's solidarity with the poor

◆

Catechetical Resources

U.S. Bishops: Pastoral Letter *Economic Justice for All* §174–178, 181, 182, 185, 188, 192

Pope Leo XIII: *The Condition of Labor,* Rerum Novarum §28–29

Pope Paul VI: *The Development of Peoples,* Populorum Progressio §43, 44, 51, 57, 61

John Paul II: *On Social Concern,* Sollicitudo Rei Socialis §41–45

CCC §1939–1942, 2443–2449

USCCA pp. 420–425, 427–428, 454–456

LITURGICAL YEAR B

ADVENT/CHRISTMAS

FIRST SUNDAY OF ADVENT

Isaiah 63:16b–27, 29b; 64:2–7

Yet, O LORD, you are our father;
we are the clay and you the potter:
we are all the work of your hands.

Apprenticeship Activity

Do small Christian communities meet regularly in the parish? These groups meet weekly to be fashioned by God into more caring, more loving communities formed in God's word. Arrange for the apprentices to visit these groups and later report on what they experienced.

Christian Formation

Small Christian communities

Catechetical Resources

Find support materials from the North American Forum for Small Faith Communities by visiting its Web site at www.nafscc.org
USCCA pp. 116–121

SECOND SUNDAY OF ADVENT

2 Peter 3:8–14

Therefore, beloved, since you await these things, be eager to be found
without spot or blemish before him, at peace.

Apprenticeship Activity

If the parish schedules a communal celebration of the sacrament of reconciliation, invite the apprentices to attend. If one or a few of the candidates will soon be welcomed into full communion, this might be their opportunity to celebrate the sacrament. (Catechumens never celebrate this sacrament before their baptism, of course.) Consider inviting one or two parishioners who celebrated the sacrament to share their experience of its healing power.

Christian Formation

Conversion and reconciliation

Catechetical Resources

Rite of Penance, Introduction
CCC §1422–1460, 1848–1876
USCCA pp. 233–247

THIRD SUNDAY OF ADVENT

Isaiah 61:1–2a, 10–11

He has sent me to bring glad tidings to the poor,
to heal the brokenhearted.

Apprenticeship Activity

Does the parish support its own or a local food pantry? Does the parish assist in the distribution of meals to the hungry? This is an ideal time to arrange for the apprentices to take part in this ministry.

Christian Formation

Church's solidarity with the poor

◆

Catechetical Resources

U.S. Bishops: Pastoral Letter *Economic Justice for All* §174–178, 181, 182, 185, 188, 192

Pope Paul VI: *The Development of Peoples*, Populorum Progressio §43, 44, 51, 57, 61, 73, 76

John Paul II: *On Social Concern*, Sollicitudo Rei Socialis §17, 41–45

Catholic Relief Services' Web site has excellent resources: www.crs.org

CCC §1939–1942, 2443–2449

USCCA pp. 420–425, 427–428, 454–456

FOURTH SUNDAY OF ADVENT

Luke 1:26–38

"And behold, Elizabeth, your relative,
has also conceived a son in her old age."

Apprenticeship Activity

Does the parish have an "Elizabeth Ministry," an outreach ministry to women in their childbearing years? If so, connect the apprentices (particularly the women) with those who provide this ministry in the parish.

Christian Formation

Dignity of human life, Christian motherhood

◆

Catechetical Resources

For support materials, Elizabeth Ministry International has an excellent Web site: www.elizabethministry.com

CCC §2222–2233

USCCA pp. 310, 387–402

CHRISTMAS
Luke 2:1–14
She wrapped him in swaddling clothes and laid him in a manger,
because there was no room for them in the inn.

Apprenticeship Activity

Does the parish have an active outreach program to assist the homeless? Does the parish Saint Vincent de Paul Society or other organization assist those who have difficulty paying their utility bills? Invite the apprentices to become involved in this critical ministry.

Christian Formation

Church's solidarity with the poor and migrants

◆

Catechetical Resources

Pope Paul VI: *The Development of Peoples*, Populorum Progressio §67–69
Pope John XXIII: *Pacem in Terris* §103–106
Catholic Relief Services' Web site has excellent resources: www.catholicrelief.org
The United States Conference of Catholic Bishops' Department of Migration and Refugee Services provides background materials and action alerts: www.usccb.org/mrs
CCC §1939–1942, 2443–2449
USCCA pp. 420–425, 427–428, 454–456

THE HOLY FAMILY OF JESUS, MARY, AND JOSEPH
Hebrews 11:8, 11–12, 17–19
By faith Abraham obeyed when we was called to go out to a place that
he was to receive as an inheritance; he went out, not knowing where he was to go.

Apprenticeship Activity

Are there vowed religious working on the pastoral staff or residing within the parish? Often these men and women, in their response to God's call, have been summoned to faraway places–not knowing anything about these places–yet they responded in faithfulness. Invite one or more of these people to a session to share their "Abraham" experiences.

Christian Formation

Consecrated life

◆

Catechetical Resources

The United States Conference of Catholic Bishops' Department for Consecrated Life provides background materials: www.usccb.org/consecratedlife
CCC §914–933
USCCA p. 135

THE SOLEMNITY OF THE BLESSED VIRGIN MARY, THE MOTHER OF GOD

Luke 2:16–21
And Mary kept all these things, reflecting on them in her heart.

Apprenticeship Activity

What ministry does the parish provide for young mothers? If such a ministry exists, invite those who extend care to these young women to a session to share their experiences with the apprentices. Perhaps invite any young mothers who are apprentices to attend a meeting of the young mothers group.

Christian Formation

Dignity of human life, Christian motherhood

◆

Catechetical Resources

For support materials, Elizabeth Ministry International has an excellent Web site: www.elizabethministry.com
CCC §2221–2231
USCCA pp. 310, 387–402

THE EPIPHANY OF THE LORD

Matthew 2:1–12
Then they opened their treasures and offered him gifts of gold, frankincense, and myrrh.

Apprenticeship Activity

The magi are examples of generous giving. Does the parish have a stewardship committee comprising people who have embraced a stewardship way of life? Invite them to inspire the apprentices with their own stories of how they live lives of good stewardship. Don't be afraid to ask these good people to be very concrete about their giving. Apprentices often have questions about appropriate giving to their parish. Many parishes do not wait until initiation to invite the apprentices to begin giving to the parish. Be sure to explain the "envelope" system at this time!

Christian Formation

Stewardship

◆

Catechetical Resources

U.S. Bishops: *Our Hearts Were Burning Within Us: A Pastoral Plan for Adult Faith Formation* in the United States §71, 122
The International Catholic Stewardship Council has excellent resources on its Web site: www.catholicstewardship.org
USCCA pp. 450–455

THE BAPTISM OF THE LORD

Isaiah 55:1–11
. . . my word shall not return to me void,
but shall do my will,
achieving the end for which I sent it.

Apprenticeship Activity

Invite some of the parish ministers of the word (lectors, people who lead children's Liturgy of the Word) to share their ministry experiences. If the parish lectors meet weekly to prepare the Sunday readings, invite the apprentices to attend this meeting.

Christian Formation

The word of God

◆

Catechetical Resources

U.S. Bishops: *Fulfilled in Your Hearing:*
  The Homily in the Sunday Assembly
Lectionary for Mass, Introduction
CCC §2653–2655
USCCA pp. 175, 177, 218

LENT

During Lent, if a parish has two "tracks," one for the elect and another for catechumens and candidates who will not celebrate the sacraments until the following year, the following ideas may be used with those bypassing the sacraments. The elect will be on their own journey preparing for, celebrating, and reflecting upon the celebration of the scrutinies.

FIRST SUNDAY OF LENT

Mark 1:12–15
The Spirit drove Jesus out into the desert, and he remained in the desert for forty days.

Apprenticeship Activity

Is there a retreat house or diocesan spiritual center in your area? Schedule a visit, meet with the staff, and perhaps arrange a mini-retreat there with the apprentices.

Christian Formation

Contemplative prayer

◆

Catechetical Resources

CCC §2559–2565, 2691, 2705–2719
USCCA pp. 300–301, 473–474, 477, 479, 490–491

SECOND SUNDAY OF LENT

Genesis 22:1–2, 9a, 10–13, 15–18
God put Abraham to the test.

Apprenticeship Activity

Is there someone in the parish who, despite tremendous trials, has shown an abundance of faith? Invite that person to share that story with the apprentices.

Christian Formation

Persistence in prayer, faith in the midst of trials

◆

Catechetical Resources

Lives of the saints
CCC §2729–2731
USCCA pp. 476–480

THIRD SUNDAY OF LENT

Exodus 20:1–3, 7–8, 12–17
You shall not have other gods besides me.

Christian Formation

"I am the Lord, your God":
The Ten Commandments

◆

Catechetical Resources

CCC §2052–2082, 2110–2117
USCCA pp. 339–349

Apprenticeship Activity

During the regular gathering of apprentices, have them watch one half-hour television program. As they view the program and the commercials, ask them if they recognize any "gods" that the program or the advertising seem to be creating.

FOURTH SUNDAY OF LENT

Psalm 137:1–2, 3, 4–5, 6
By the streams of Babylon
we sat and wept
when we remembered Zion.

Christian Formation

Corporal works of mercy:
Burying the dead

◆

Catechetical Resources

Corporal works of mercy
CCC §1681–1683, 2447–2448
USCCA pp. 158–160, 508

Apprenticeship Activity

Are there parishioners who regularly attend wakes/visitations at funeral homes on behalf of the parish? Invite apprentices (perhaps in smaller numbers) to accompany those from the parish who attend wakes/visitations. Remind them that this ministry is one of the corporal works of mercy.

FIFTH SUNDAY OF LENT

John 12:20–33

"And when I am lifted up from the earth, I will draw everyone to myself."
He said this indicating the kind of death he would die.

Apprenticeship Activity

Catholics honor the memory of the crucifixion of Christ in a number of ways. Many people wear a cross or crucifix as a piece of jewelry. Catholics also place crosses and crucifixes in their cars, at their desks, and in their homes. This might be a good opportunity to visit the various places on the parish property where crosses and crucifixes have been placed. Be sure to research this in advance. Crosses can sometimes be found on parish stationery, on sacred vessels and liturgical books, on vestments, on liturgical linens, on baptism fonts. Invite the apprentices to lift and carry the parish's processional cross(es). This is a wonderful preparation for next Sunday's celebration of the Lord's passion.

Christian Formation

The cross of Christ

◆

Catechetical Resources

CCC §616–618
USCCA pp. 91–93

PALM SUNDAY OF THE LORD'S PASSION

Mark 14:1 – 15:47

A woman came with an alabaster jar of perfumed oil.

Apprenticeship Activity

During Holy Week, members of the parish will attend the (arch)diocesan Chrism Mass, celebrated by the bishop. Before last year's oils are disposed of, invite the apprentices to visit the ambry where the oils are stored. If a parish priest will anoint someone with the oil of the sick sometime during the week, invite a few of the apprentices to accompany him for the celebration of the sacrament. If the priest knows of someone who is in need of this sacrament, someone who is mobile, consider inviting that person into an initiation session to experience the anointing surrounded by the apprentices.

Christian Formation

Holy oils, anointing of the sick

◆

Catechetical Resources

CCC §1499–1532
Rite of Anointing and Pastoral Care of the Sick, Introduction
USCCA pp. 249–259

EASTER TRIDUUM

There is no better way to form people in the Catholic faith than to walk with them through the celebration of the Triduum. Invite them to take part in the washing of feet on Holy Thursday, the veneration of the cross on Good Friday, and the celebration of the initiation sacraments at the Easter Vigil. Invite the apprentices to make this three-day festival a retreat experience.

SECOND SUNDAY OF EASTER

Acts 4:32–35
There was no needy person among them,
for those who owned property or houses would sell them,
bring the proceeds of the sale, and put them at the feet of the apostles,
and they were distributed to each according to need.

Apprenticeship Activity

Now that spring is in full swing, invite the apprentices to organize a garage sale. Encourage them to go through their clothes closets and collect everything that has not been worn in one year. Invite them to take an honest inventory of their household possessions with an eye toward keeping those "things" that are essential, and setting aside items for the yard sale. All of the items could then be assembled, perhaps at the home of one of the apprentices, or perhaps on the parish property. Schedule the yard sale, and be sure that people know that all proceeds will be donated to the parish or to a specific ministry or charity sponsored by the parish.

Christian Formation

Church's solidarity with the poor

◆

Catechetical Resources

U.S. Bishops: Pastoral Letter *Economic Justice for All*
Pope John XXIII: *On Christianity and Social Progress*, Mater et Magistra §4, 6
Pope Paul VI: *The Development of Peoples*, Populorum Progressio §21, 23, 24
John Paul II: *On Social Concern,* Sollicitudo Rei Socialis §42
Catholic Relief Services' Web site has excellent resources: www.crs.org
CCC §1939–1942, 2443–2449
USCCA pp. 420–425, 427–428, 454–456

THIRD SUNDAY OF EASTER

Luke 24:35–48
While they were still speaking about this,
he stood in their midst and said to them, "Peace be with you."

Christian Formation

Catholic social teaching on peace and justice

◆

Catechetical Resources

U.S. Bishops: *The Challenge of Peace:*
  God's Promise and Our Response,
  A Pastoral Letter on War and Peace
  §27–29, 44–54
Pope John XXIII: *Pacem in Terris*
  §166–171
CCC §1928–1948, 2302–2317
USCCA pp. 420–425

Apprenticeship Activity

Does the parish have a peace and justice committee? Are there parishioners who organize letter-writing campaigns that address issues of peace with legislators? Invite these people to a session and have them speak about their experiences and commitment to peace. Perhaps they can organize a letter-writing campaign that addresses these issues with the apprentices.

FOURTH SUNDAY OF EASTER

John 10:11–18
Jesus said: "I am the good shepherd."

Christian Formation

The ministry of the bishop

◆

Catechetical Resources

CCC §1554–1561
USCCA pp. 265–266

Apprenticeship Activity

Invite your diocesan bishop to a meeting with the apprentices. The neophytes could be invited as well. Be sure to secure the bishop's presence well in advance, since his calendar is probably very full. Invite him to share his experience as the shepherd of the diocese and how his ministry is inspired by the example of Jesus, the Good Shepherd.

B

FIFTH SUNDAY OF EASTER

John 15:1–8

"I am the vine, you are the branches."

Apprenticeship Activity

The parish is a group of believers who are knitted together as a community, the "branches" on the vine. Is there a party, dance, or festival planned in the parish at this time of year? Apprentices could be invited to help plan this kind of community-building event.

Christian Formation

Parish as community of believers

◆

Catechetical Resources

CCC §2179
USCCA pp. 121–122, 134–135

SIXTH SUNDAY OF EASTER

1 John 4:7–10

Beloved, let us love one another, because love is of God.

Apprenticeship Activity

Does the parish have a ministry to those preparing for marriage? Invite those involved in this ministry to share their experience with the apprentices. Why not invite one of the engaged couples involved in marriage preparation to accompany these ministers to a session? Allow the apprentices to experience this ministry firsthand.

Christian Formation

Christian marriage

◆

Catechetical Resources

Rite of Marriage, Introduction
CCC §1601–1666
USCCA pp. 277–292

THE ASCENSION OF THE LORD

Ephesians 4:1–13
And he gave some as apostles, others as prophets, others as evangelists,
others as pastors and teachers.

Apprenticeship Activity

Invite the apprentices to attend a religion class in your Catholic school or a class in your religious education program. Let them become the "teachers" for the session. Invite them to share their faith experience with the young people gathered for formation.

Christian Formation

The teaching office of the Church

◆

Catechetical Resources

General Directory for Catechesis §78, 79
U.S. Bishops: *Our Hearts Were Burning Within Us: A Pastoral Plan for Adult Faith Formation in the United States* §68–73
CCC §426–429
USCCA pp. 133, 330

SEVENTH SUNDAY OF EASTER

Acts 1:15–17, 20a, 20c–26
For it is written in the Book of Psalms: May another take his office.

Apprenticeship Activity

Is there a seminary or house of formation located in the diocese? Does the diocese currently have seminarians in priestly formation? Is there a newly ordained priest in your parish or a nearby parish? Perhaps you could schedule a trip to the seminary. Or you could invite a seminarian to visit your parish and speak to the apprentices, focusing on the answer to the vocational call. Be sure that in this session the apprentices have the opportunity to share their own stories of having been called by God to this journey of faith.

Christian Formation

Vocation to the priesthood, the priesthood

◆

Catechetical Resources

Rites of Ordination, Introduction
The U.S. Bishops' department on Priestly Life and Ministry has an informative Web site: www.usccb.org/plm
CCC §1546–1553, 1562–1568
USCCA pp. 261–275

PENTECOST

John 20:19–23
"Receive the Holy Spirit."

Apprenticeship Activity

Many parishes celebrate the sacrament of confirmation with young people during the Easter season. Invite the apprentices to attend this celebration. Or you may want to invite the confirmation catechists to a session to share their experiences of preparing young people for this sacrament of initiation. Furthermore, those who have been confirmed could be invited to a session to share their experience of preparation for the sacrament. This is a great opportunity to prepare a mystagogical catechesis on the celebration itself with these young people. Do this mystagogical catechesis at the session with apprentices.

Christian Formation

Sacrament of confirmation

Catechetical Resources

Rite of Confirmation, Introduction
CCC §1285–1321
USCCA pp. 201–211

ORDINARY TIME

THE SOLEMNITY OF THE MOST HOLY TRINITY

Matthew 28:16–20
"Go, therefore, and make disciples of all nations,
baptizing them in the name of the Father, and of the Son, and of the Holy Spirit."

Christian Formation

Sacrament of baptism

◆

Catechetical Resources

Rite of Christian Initiation of Adults
  (RCIA) or *Sacramentary,* Blessing of
  Water for the Easter Vigil
RCIA, Introduction
Rite of Baptism for Children,
  Introduction
CCC §1213–1284
USCCA pp. 181–199

Apprenticeship Activity

Does the parish have baptism preparation sessions for parents and godparents of newborns? Invite the apprentices to attend a baptism preparation session.

THE SOLEMNITY OF THE MOST HOLY BODY AND BLOOD OF CHRIST

Mark 14:12–16, 22–26
Jesus' disciples said to him,
"Where do you want us to go and prepare for you to eat the Passover?"

Christian Formation

The parish church and its furnishings

◆

Catechetical Resources

U.S. Bishops: *Built of Living Stones: Art,*
  Architecture, and Worship

Apprenticeship Activity

This is an ideal time to invite the apprentices to assist those whose special responsibility it is to keep the church and its furnishings neat and orderly. Schedule a time when the apprentices could help clean liturgical vessels, linens, pews, reconciliation rooms, shrines, and other areas of the worship space.

SECOND SUNDAY IN ORDINARY TIME

John 1:35–42

He said to them, "Come, and you will see."

Apprenticeship Activity

The parish priest is someone who has answered the vocational call to ordained ministry. Invite your priest(s) to a session with the apprentices, not to give a theology of priesthood, but to witness to God's initial and continuing call and how this has been lived out. Invite the apprentices to share their experience of responding to God's call as well. Perhaps a tour of or an open house at the rectory could be arranged.

Christian Formation

Vocation to the priesthood, the priesthood

◆

Catechetical Resources

Rites of Ordination, Introduction
The U.S. Bishops' department on Priestly Life and Ministry has an informative Web site: www.usccb.org/plm
CCC §1546–1553, 1562–1568
USCCA pp. 261–275

THIRD SUNDAY IN ORDINARY TIME

Psalm 25:4–5, 6–7, 8–9

Teach me your ways, O Lord.

Apprenticeship Activity

Does the parish have ongoing adult education? Invite the apprentices to attend an adult education session, then reflect on that session with the rest of the group.

Christian Formation

The teaching office of the Church

◆

Catechetical Resources

General Directory for Catechesis §78, 79
U.S. Bishops: *Our Hearts Were Burning Within Us: A Pastoral Plan for Adult Faith Formation in the United States* §68–73
CCC §426–429
USCCA pp. 133, 330

FOURTH SUNDAY IN ORDINARY TIME

Psalm 95:1–2, 6–7, 7–9

Come, let us sing joyfully to the LORD.

Apprenticeship Activity

Invite the apprentices to attend a choir rehearsal, or invite the parish cantors to a session with the apprentices. Ask them to witness to their great love for music. If your parish has an organ, ask the organist to demonstrate the instrument. If the parish has a large pipe organ, invite the organist to arrange an "organ crawl" with the apprentices.

Christian Formation

Music in Catholic worship

◆

Catechetical Resources

U.S. Bishops: *Music in Catholic Worship, Liturgical Music Today*
CCC §1156–1158
USCCA pp. 171–175

FIFTH SUNDAY IN ORDINARY TIME

Mark 1:29–39

Jesus entered the house of Simon and Andrew with James and John. Simon's mother-in-law lay sick with a fever.

Apprenticeship Activity

Does the parish have an outreach to those who are confined to their homes? Arrange for apprentices to accompany ministers of care on their visits to the homebound. If the local community has a "meals-on-wheels" program, contact the organization to ask if your apprentices might assist in this program.

Christian Formation

Care for the sick

◆

Catechetical Resources

Corporal works of mercy
CCC §1500–1510, 2447–2448
USCCA pp. 225–227, 254

B

SIXTH SUNDAY IN ORDINARY TIME

Mark 1:40–45

A leper came to Jesus and kneeling down begged him and said,
"If you wish, can make me clean."

Apprenticeship Activity

Contact your diocesan Catholic Charities office and find out about the many services they offer to those in the community who are considered outcasts. Seek ways to connect apprentices with these ministries of help and outreach.

Christian Formation

Solidarity with the poor and the outcast

◆

Catechetical Resources

Pope Paul VI: *The Development of Peoples*, Populorum Progressio §67–69

John Paul II: *On Social Concern*, Sollicitudo Rei Socialis §42, 45

CCC §1939–1942, 2443–2449

USCCA pp. 420–425, 427–428, 454–456

SEVENTH SUNDAY IN ORDINARY TIME

Mark 2:1–12

Unable to get near Jesus because of the crowd,
they opened up the roof above him.
After they had broken through, they let down the mat on which the paralytic was lying.

Apprenticeship Activity

Does the parish schedule a communal celebration of the sacrament of the anointing of the sick? If so, invite the apprentices to attend the service. If not, invite the pastor and parish staff to consider scheduling such a service. Perhaps invite the pastor to anoint someone in need of the sacrament at a meeting of the apprentices.

Christian Formation

Holy oils, anointing of the sick

◆

Catechetical Resources

Rite of Anointing and Pastoral Care of the Sick, Introduction

CCC §1499–1532

USCCA pp. 249–259

EIGHTH SUNDAY IN ORDINARY TIME

Mark 2:18–22

The disciples of John and of the Pharisees were accustomed to fast.

Apprenticeship Activity

The discipline of fasting has been an important part of the lives of Christians for centuries. Too often we only think of fasting during the Lenten season. Why not choose a reason for a week-long fast, such as world peace, respect for the dignity of life, or an end to HIV-AIDS, and invite the apprentices to fast during the week, focusing on one of these causes? Perhaps on one or two days during the week lunch could consist of a simple meal of bread and water. Perhaps people are asked not to eat at a restaurant for the entire week.

Christian Formation

The discipline of fasting

◆

Catechetical Resources

CCC §1434

The U.S. Bishops' Web site has various prayers for those who are fasting: www.usccb.org/nab/fasting.htm

USCCA pp. 334–335, 518

NINTH SUNDAY IN ORDINARY TIME

Mark 2:23 – 3:6

"The sabbath was made for man, not man for the sabbath."

Apprenticeship Activity

One of the liturgical ministries vital to our Sunday celebrations is that of the parish usher or minister of hospitality who makes our "Sabbath" day one of welcome, marked with Christian hospitality. Invite the apprentices to pair up with a parish usher before Mass and assist in welcoming parishioners, helping people find seats, and assisting with the elderly and persons with disabilities.

Christian Formation

The virtue of Christian hospitality

◆

Catechetical Resources

General Instruction on the Roman Missal, Introductory Rites of Mass

TENTH SUNDAY IN ORDINARY TIME

Genesis 3:9–15

"You have eaten, then, from the tree of which I had forbidden you to eat!"

Christian Formation

Sacrament of baptism, original sin

◆

Catechetical Resources

Rite of Christian Initiation of Adults (RCIA) or *Sacramentary,* Blessing of Water for the Easter Vigil
RCIA, Introduction
Rite of Baptism for Children, Introduction
CCC §1213–1284
USCCA pp. 67–75

Apprenticeship Activity

Today's first reading recalls the story of the fall of Adam and Eve, as well as our inheritance of this original sin. Baptism completely wipes out original sin. Invite the apprentices to attend a parish celebration of infant baptism.

ELEVENTH SUNDAY IN ORDINARY TIME

Ezekiel 17:22–24

And all the trees of the field shall know
that I, the LORD,
Bring low the high tree,
lift high the lowly tree,
Wither up the green tree,
and make the withered tree bloom.

Christian Formation

God's creation reveals God's presence, respect for God's creation

◆

Catechetical Resources

CCC §341, 2415–2418
USCCA pp. 3–4, 67–68

Apprenticeship Activity

The wonders of creation reveal the splendor of God. Contemplating the beauty of God's creation can lead one to a deeper awareness of God. Too often we simply walk or drive by one of the most intricate and beautiful of all God's creatures: the tree. Schedule a visit to a local park, arboretum, or forested area. Invite the apprentices to ponder the beauty of the tree. Invite them to pray in thanksgiving for all that God has so wonderfully made for us in this garden of earth.

TWELFTH SUNDAY IN ORDINARY TIME

Mark 4:35–41

He woke up, rebuked the wind, and said to the sea, "Quiet! Be still!

Apprenticeship Activity

Unfortunately, the reality of terrorism around the world causes many of us to live in fear for our own safety and the safety of our children. Praying for an end to terrorism and the establishment of a true and lasting peace can help ease our fears and bring an end to this kind of horrible violence. Why not ask the apprentices to create a prayer service for peace and an end to terrorism? Perhaps members of the parish liturgy planning committee could assist the apprentices as mentors. This prayer service for peace could be placed on the parish calendar, with all parishioners invited to attend.

Christian Formation

Preparing liturgical prayer

◆

Catechetical Resources

Worship preparation materials
  widely available
CCC §2844
USCCA pp. 476–477

THIRTEENTH SUNDAY IN ORDINARY TIME

Mark 5:21–43

"My daughter is at the point of death.
Please, come and lay hands on her that she may get well and live."

Apprenticeship Activity

Are there parishioners caring for the terminally ill in hospitals, nursing centers, or through hospice? Perhaps a few of the apprentices could be paired with these parishioners for a visit to someone who is terminally ill, assisting in whatever way is needed.

Christian Formation

Church's ministry of healing

◆

Catechetical Resources

*Rite of Anointing and Pastoral Care of
  the Sick,* Introduction
CCC §1499–1532
USCCA pp. 249–259

FOURTEENTH SUNDAY IN ORDINARY TIME

2 Corinthians 12:7–10
*Therefore, I am content with weaknesses, insults, hardships,
persecutions, and constraints, for the sake of Christ; for when I am weak, then I am strong.*

Christian Formation

Sickness in the Christian context

◆

Catechetical Resources

*Rite of Anointing and Pastoral Care of
the Sick,* Introduction
CCC §1499–1532
USCCA pp. 251–252, 256

Apprenticeship Activity

Often people living with chronic illness become signs of hope and strength, even in the face of constant sickness and pain. Invite one or more people living with chronic illness into a session to share with the apprentices their hope and courage.

FIFTEENTH SUNDAY IN ORDINARY TIME

Mark 6:7–13
Jesus summoned the Twelve and began to send them out two by two.

Christian Formation

Christian hospitality, welcome, forming community

◆

Catechetical Resources

CCC §2179
USCCA pp. 134–135

Apprenticeship Activity

Parishes often have numerous ways that members visit each other. If a parish census is to be taken, invite the apprentices to become involved as census-takers. Many parishes schedule visits to the homes of new parishioners. Invite the apprentices to accompany a member of the parish welcoming committee in a visit to the home of new parishioner.

SIXTEENTH SUNDAY IN ORDINARY TIME

Mark 6:30–34

"Come away by yourselves to a deserted place and rest a while."

Apprenticeship Activity

Does the parish schedule a parish retreat during the year? If so, invite the apprentices to attend. Or arrange for a special retreat solely for the apprentices and their sponsors and godparents. Arrange a visit to a local retreat center or center for meditation and contemplation.

Christian Formation

Contemplative prayer

◆

Catechetical Resources

CCC §2559–2565, 2691, 2705–2719
USCCA pp. 300–301, 473–474, 477, 479, 490–491

SEVENTEENTH SUNDAY IN ORDINARY TIME

John 6:1–15

"Where can we buy enough food for them to eat?"

Apprenticeship Activity

If the parish has a food pantry for the poor, ask those who run it what kinds of food they currently need the most. If the parish does not have a pantry, contact a parish that does have one or search for one in your local community. Ascertain which foods are most needed. Then send the apprentices out on a shopping spree. Invite them to purchase this much-needed food from their own funds, carefully figuring out what they can afford. Then collect these items and have the apprentices deliver the food to the pantry.

Christian Formation

Church's solidarity with the poor

◆

Catechetical Resources

Pope Leo XIII: *The Condition of Labor*, Rerum Novarum §24, 29, 30
Pope John XXIII: *On Christianity and Social Progress*, Mater et Magistra §121
Pope Paul VI: *The Development of Peoples*, Populorum Progressio §75
John Paul II: *On Social Concern*, Sollicitudo Rei Socialis §47
Catholic Relief Services' Web site has excellent resources: www.crs.org
CCC §1939–1942, 2443–2449
USCCA pp. 420–425, 427–428, 454–456

EIGHTEENTH SUNDAY IN ORDINARY TIME

John 6:24–35
*"I am the bread of life; whoever comes to me will never hunger,
and whoever believes in me will never thirst."*

Apprenticeship Activity

Invite some extraordinary ministers of Communion
to a session with the apprentices. Ask these ministers
to talk about their devotion to the Holy Eucharist and
how their ministry helps deepen their own love for the
Eucharist. The session might include a hands-on "how
to go to Communion" lesson, using unconsecrated hosts
and wine. Make this session spiritual and practical.
Adults who receive their First Holy Communion are
often confused and anxious about how to create a
throne from the palms of their hands, whether or not
they should take the Communion cup completely, when
to say "Amen," and so on. A session like this calms their
fears and can assist in clearing up confusion.

Christian Formation
Reception of the Holy
Eucharist

◆

Catechetical Resources
*General Instruction of the
Roman Missal*
CCC §1322–1419
USCCA pp. 224–225, 366–368

NINETEENTH SUNDAY IN ORDINARY TIME

John 6:41–51
"I am the living bread that came down from heaven."

Christian Formation
The Eucharist

◆

Catechetical Resources
*General Instruction of the
Roman Missal*
CCC §1322–1419
USCCA pp. 213–232

Apprenticeship Activity

Some parishes invite parishioners to bake the bread
to be used at Mass, using recipes approved by the
Church. Invite the apprentices to the home of one of
these parishioners for an evening of eucharistic bread
baking.

B

TWENTIETH SUNDAY IN ORDINARY TIME

Ephesians 5:15–20

Be filled with the Spirit, addressing one another in psalms and hymns and spiritual songs, singing and playing to the Lord in your hearts.

Christian Formation

Music in Catholic worship

◆

Catechetical Resources

U.S. Bishops: *Music in Catholic Worship, Liturgical Music Today*
CCC §1156–1158
USCCA pp. 171, 175

Apprenticeship Activity

Are there parishioners who assist in the music ministry of the parish by playing an instrument? Invite them to a session with the apprentices. Ask them to share what it means for them to give of their talent to the parish. If some of the apprentices play a musical instrument, invite them to bring it to this session. Perhaps they can be given some of the liturgical music used in the parish. They could then learn it and begin ministering to the apprentices and to the wider worshiping assembly during the Liturgy of the Word at Sunday Mass.

TWENTY-FIRST SUNDAY IN ORDINARY TIME

Ephesians 5:21–32

Husbands, love your wives.

Christian Formation

Christian marriage

◆

Catechetical Resources

Rite of Marriage, Introduction
CCC §1601–1666
USCCA pp. 277–292

Apprenticeship Activity

Does the parish have programs for marriage enrichment, like Worldwide Marriage Encounter? Invite the spouses of the apprentices to attend a session during which some of those involved in marriage ministry in the parish speak about these enrichment programs. If no such program exists, invite a few couples who have been married for fifty years or more to relate their experience of Christian marriage.

B

TWENTY-SECOND SUNDAY IN ORDINARY TIME

James 1:17–18, 21b–22, 27
Humbly welcome the word that has been planted in you and is able to save your souls.

Apprenticeship Activity

Invite some of the parish lectors to a session with the apprentices. Ask them to share their love for the scripture and how the word inspires them in their daily lives. Perhaps the session could include a trip into the church. Invite the lectors to show and explain how biblical readings are organized into the Lectionary for Mass. Perhaps the apprentices could be invited to proclaim a reading from the Lectionary at the ambo.

Christian Formation

The word of God

◆

Catechetical Resources

U.S. Bishops: *Fulfilled in Your Hearing: The Homily in the Sunday Assembly*
Lectionary for Mass, Introduction
CCC §2653–2655
USCCA pp. 175, 177, 218

TWENTY-THIRD SUNDAY IN ORDINARY TIME

Mark 7:31–37
"He makes the deaf hear and the mute speak."

Apprenticeship Activity

Many parishes provide sign language interpretation at Sunday Mass for those who are deaf. Invite a few of these sign-language interpreters to your session with the apprentices. Ask them to share how their ministry of the word has brought them to a deeper appreciation of the scriptures. Perhaps they can be invited to teach the apprentices a few simple liturgical expressions in sign language, such as "And also with you," "Amen," and "Alleluia."

Christian Formation

The languages of the liturgy

◆

Catechetical Resources

Sign language resources

TWENTY-FOURTH SUNDAY IN ORDINARY TIME

James 2:14–18

*If a brother or sister has nothing to wear and has no food for the day,
and one of you says to them, "Go in peace, keep warm, and eat well,"
but you do not give them the necessities of the body, what good is it?*

Apprenticeship Activity

Consider inviting the apprentices to organize a clothing drive to assist the poor. Among other things, they will need to learn how to generate announcements at Sunday Mass, how to arrange to have announcements placed in the parish bulletin, how to arrange for parish storage space for the clothing, and how to arrange to get the clothing to those who need it.

Christian Formation

Church's solidarity with the poor

◆

Catechetical Resources

U.S. Bishops: Pastoral Letter *Economic Justice for All*

Pope Leo XIII: *The Condition of Labor*, Rerum Novarum §24, 28–30

Pope John XXIII: *On Christianity and Social Progress*, Mater et Magistra §159, 160

Pope Paul VI: *The Development of Peoples*, Populorum Progressio §43, 44, 51, 57, 61, 73, 76

John Paul II: *On Social Concern*, Sollicitudo Rei Socialis §17

Catholic Relief Services' Web site has excellent resources: www.crs.org

CCC §1939–1942, 2443–2449

USCCA pp. 420–425, 427–428, 454–456

TWENTY-FIFTH SUNDAY IN ORDINARY TIME

James 3:16 – 4:3

And the fruit of righteousness is sown in peace for those who cultivate peace.

Apprenticeship Activity

Does the parish have a peace and justice committee? Invite members of that committee to meet with the apprentices to solicit help with a peace project. Consider contacting Pax Christi International to find ways to work locally for peace.

Christian Formation

Catholic social teaching on peace and justice

◆

Catechetical Resources

U.S. Bishops: *The Challenge of Peace: God's Promise and Our Response, A Pastoral Letter on War and Peace* §326–329, 27–29

Pope John XXIII: *Pacem in Terris* §35, 36, 166–172

Pax Christi's Web site: www.paxchristiusa.org

CCC §1928–1948, 2302–2317

USCCA pp. 420–425

TWENTY-SIXTH SUNDAY IN ORDINARY TIME

Psalm 19:8, 10, 12–13, 14
The law of the LORD is perfect,
refreshing the soul.

Apprenticeship Activity

Arrange a visit to the (arch)diocesan pastoral center or chancery. Schedule a meeting with those who work in the marriage tribunal and with those who deal with issues of canon law. This session could be designed to help apprentices understand the Church's teaching on marriage.

Christian Formation

Marriage tribunal, canon law

◆

Catechetical Resources

General Introduction to the *Code of Canon Law*
Rite of Marriage, Introduction
CCC §1601–1666
USCCA pp. 381–382, 403–416

TWENTY-SEVENTH SUNDAY IN ORDINARY TIME

Mark 10:2–16
"Let the children come to me; do not prevent them,
for the kingdom of God belongs to such as these."

Apprenticeship Activity

Contact the parish director of religious education to arrange for a visit of the apprentices to a religious education class for young children. Perhaps the apprentices could be assigned to take part in actually teaching the class. Sharing from their own new experience of the faith, this session just might lead them to a future of ministry to children of the parish!

Christian Formation

The teaching office of the Church

◆

Catechetical Resources

General Directory for Catechesis §78, 79
U.S. Bishops: *Our Hearts Were Burning Within Us: A Pastoral Plan for Adult Faith Formation in the United States* §68–73
CCC §426–429
USCCA pp. 133, 330

TWENTY-EIGHTH SUNDAY IN ORDINARY TIME

Wisdom 7:7–11

I prayed, and prudence was given me;
I pleaded, and the spirit of wisdom came to me.

Christian Formation

Prayer

◆

Catechetical Resources

Liturgy of the Hours, Introduction
CCC §2558ff
USCCA pp. 461–495

Apprenticeship Activity

Is there a group in the parish that regularly gathers for prayer? Is evening prayer regularly scheduled? Rather than simply teaching the apprentices about prayer, why not invite them to pray with those who do so regularly?

TWENTY-NINTH SUNDAY IN ORDINARY TIME

Mark 10:35–45

"For the Son of Man did not come to be served
but to serve and to give his life as a ransom for many."

Christian Formation

Church's solidarity with the poor

◆

Catechetical Resources

U.S. Bishops: Pastoral Letter *Economic Justice for All* §174–178, 181, 182, 185, 188, 192
Pope Leo XIII: *The Condition of Labor*, Rerum Novarum §28–30
Pope John XXIII: *On Christianity and Social Progress,* Mater et Magistra §159, 160
Pope Paul VI: *The Development of Peoples,* Populorum Progressio §43, 44, 51, 57, 61, 73, 76
John Paul II: *On Social Concern,* Sollicitudo Rei Socialis §17
Catholic Relief Services' Web site has excellent resources: www.crs.org
CCC §1939–1942, 2443–2449
USCCA pp. 420–425, 427–428, 454–456

Apprenticeship Activity

Is there a soup kitchen or homeless shelter in the community that regularly serves meals to the needy? Contact the organization and arrange for the apprentices to serve one of those meals.

THIRTIETH SUNDAY IN ORDINARY TIME

Mark 10:46–52

Jesus told him, "Go your way; your faith has saved you."
Immediately he received his sight and followed him on the way.

Apprenticeship Activity

Does your parish or another in your area regularly schedule healing services? Invite the apprentices to attend a healing service.

Christian Formation

Church's ministry of healing

◆

Catechetical Resources

Rite of Anointing and Pastoral Care of the Sick, Introduction
CCC §1499–1532
USCCA pp. 251–259

THIRTY-FIRST SUNDAY IN ORDINARY TIME

Mark 12:28b–34

"You shall love your neighbor as yourself."

Apprenticeship Activity

Does the parish have a Saint Vincent de Paul Society? Often this group of parishioners extends help to the elderly in the parish. Invite the members of the society to a session in order to schedule opportunities for the apprentices to become involved in this ministry to the elderly.

Christian Formation

Dignity of the human person, especially the elderly

◆

Catechetical Resources

Pope John Paul II, *The Gospel of Life, Evangelium Vitae* §94
USCCA pp. 43, 337–338, 377–378

THIRTY-SECOND SUNDAY IN ORDINARY TIME

Mark 12:38–44

"Amen, I say to you, this poor widow put in more than all the other contributors to the treasury. For they have all contributed from their surplus wealth, but she, from her poverty, has contributed all she had, her whole livelihood."

Apprenticeship Activity

Giving of our treasure is a foundational pillar of living the life of a good steward. Does the parish have a stewardship committee? Invite a member of that committee to witness to the power of stewardship. Invite the apprentices to a meeting of the parish finance committee so that they can see firsthand the needs of the parish and the difference their own stewardship can make.

Christian Formation

Stewardship

◆

Catechetical Resources

U.S. Bishops: *Our Hearts Were Burning Within Us: A Pastoral Plan for Adult Faith Formation in the United States* §71, 122

The International Catholic Stewardship Council has excellent resources on its Web site: www.catholicstewardship.org

USCCA pp. 450–455

THIRTY-THIRD SUNDAY IN ORDINARY TIME

Hebrews 10:11–14, 18

Every priest stands daily at his ministry.

Apprenticeship Activity

Invite your parish priest to administer to the catechumens the anointing with the oil of catechumens. Take this opportunity to ask your priest to share with the apprentices the tasks that take up his daily life. Perhaps this session could include a tour of the parish rectory.

Christian Formation

Oil of catechumens, the priesthood

◆

Catechetical Resources

Rites of Ordination, Introduction
CCC §1539–1554
USCCA p. 185

THIRTY-FOURTH OR LAST SUNDAY IN ORDINARY TIME
THE SOLEMNITY OF OUR LORD JESUS CHRIST THE KING

Daniel 7:13–14
His dominion is an everlasting dominion
that shall not be taken away.

Christian Formation

Persistence in prayer, faith in the midst of trials

◆

Catechetical Resources

Lives of the saints
CCC §2729–2731
USCCA pp. 476–480

Apprenticeship Activity

Invite an elderly member of your parish to come to a session to share with the apprentices his or her own story of steadfastness in faith over the years. Perhaps invite someone who has been through many hardships–possibly the death of a spouse–and has remained faithful through it all.

LITURGICAL YEAR

ADVENT/CHRISTMAS

FIRST SUNDAY OF ADVENT

1 Thessalonians 3:12 – 4:2

For you know what instructions we gave you through the Lord Jesus.

Apprenticeship Activity

Invite those who coordinate religious education in the parish to a session with the apprentices. Invite them to share their experience of handing on the tradition of the Church to those entrusted to their catechetical care.

Christian Formation

The content of the Catholic faith

◆

Catechetical Resources

General Directory for Catechesis §92–102

SECOND SUNDAY OF ADVENT

Luke 3:1–6

*John went throughout the whole region of the Jordan,
proclaiming a baptism of repentance
for the forgiveness of sins.*

Apprenticeship Activity

Does the parish have an evangelization committee? If so, invite members to share their experiences with the apprentices. Consider inviting the apprentices to a meeting of this parish committee.

Christian Formation

Evangelization

◆

Catechetical Resources

Pope Paul VI: *On Evangelization in the Modern World*, Evangelii Nuntiandi
Pope John Paul II: *The New Evangelization*
U.S. Bishops: *Our Hearts Were Burning Within Us: A Pastoral Plan for Adult Faith Formation in the United States*
USCCA pp. 16–17, 134–136, 502

THIRD SUNDAY OF ADVENT

Luke 3:10–18

He said to them in reply, "Whoever has two cloaks
should share with the person who has none."

Apprenticeship Activity

Consider inviting the apprentices to organize a
clothing drive to assist the poor. Among other
things, they will need to learn how to generate
announcements at Sunday Mass, how to arrange to
have announcements placed in the parish bulletin,
how to arrange for parish storage space for the
clothing, and how to arrange to get the clothing to
those who need it.

Christian Formation

Church's solidarity with the poor

Catechetical Resources

U.S. Bishops: Pastoral Letter *Economic
  Justice for All* §174–178
Pope Leo XIII: *The Condition of Labor*,
  Rerum Novarum §28–30
Pope John XXIII: *On Christianity and
  Social Progress*, Mater et Magistra
  §159, 160
Pope Paul VI: *The Development of
  Peoples*, Populorum Progressio
  §43, 44, 51, 57, 61, 73, 76
John Paul II: *On Social Concern*,
  Sollicitudo Rei Socialis §7, 41–45
Catholic Relief Services' Web site has
  excellent resources: www.crs.org
CCC §1939–1942, 2443–2449
USCCA pp. 420–425, 427–428, 454–456

FOURTH SUNDAY OF ADVENT

Luke 1:39–45

Mary set out and traveled to the hill country
in haste to a town of Judah,
where she entered the house of Zechariah and greeted Elizabeth.

Apprenticeship Activity

Does the parish have an "Elizabeth Ministry," an
outreach ministry to women in their childbearing years?
If so, connect the apprentices (particularly the women)
with those who provide this ministry in the parish.

Christian Formation

Dignity of human life, Christian
motherhood

Catechetical Resources

For support materials, Elizabeth
  Ministry International has
  an excellent Web site:
  www.elizabethministry.com
CCC §2222–2233
USCCA pp. 310, 387–402

CHRISTMAS

Luke 2:1–14

*She wrapped him in swaddling clothes and laid him in a manger,
because there was no room for them in the inn.*

Apprenticeship Activity

Does the parish have an active outreach program to assist the homeless? Does the parish Saint Vincent de Paul Society or other organization assist those who have difficulty paying their utility bills? Invite the apprentices to become involved in this critical ministry.

Christian Formation

Church's solidarity with the poor and migrants

◆

Catechetical Resources

U.S. Bishops: Pastoral Letter *Economic Justice for All*

Pope John XXIII: *Peace on Earth*, Pacem in Terris §103–106

Pope Paul VI: *The Development of Peoples*, Populorum Progressio §67–69

Catholic Relief Services' Web site has excellent resources: www.crs.org

The United States Conference of Catholic Bishops' Department of Migration and Refugee Services provides background materials and action alerts: www.usccb.org/mrs

CCC §1939–1942, 2443–2449

USCCA pp. 420–425, 427–428, 454–456

THE HOLY FAMILY OF JESUS, MARY, AND JOSEPH

Luke 2:41–52

And his mother kept all these things in her heart.

Apprenticeship Activity

What ministry does the parish provide for young mothers? If such a ministry exists, invite those who extend care to these young women to a session to share their experiences with the apprentices. Perhaps invite any young mothers who are apprentices to attend a meeting of the young mothers group.

Christian Formation

Dignity of human life, Christian motherhood

◆

Catechetical Resources

For support materials, Elizabeth Ministry International has an excellent Web site: www.elizabethministry.com

CCC §2221–2231

USCCA pp. 310, 387–402

THE SOLEMNITY OF THE BLESSED VIRGIN MARY, THE MOTHER OF GOD

Luke 2:16–21

*The shepherds went in haste to Bethlehem and found Mary and Joseph,
and the infant lying in the manger.*

Apprenticeship Activity

Is there a couple in the parish who have very recently experienced the birth of their first child? Perhaps arrange a visit with a small number of the apprentices to this new family's home. Ask the new parents to share their experience of the birth of their child through the perspective of faith.

Christian Formation

Wonder at God's creation

◆

Catechetical Resources

CCC §341
USCCA pp. 3–4, 67–68

THE EPIPHANY OF THE LORD

Matthew 2:1–12

*And having been warned in a dream not to return to Herod,
they departed for their country by another way.*

Apprenticeship Activity

Following this scripture passage comes the description of Herod's slaughter of the Holy Innocents in an effort to kill the child Jesus. Does the parish or diocese have an active Respect Life group that works to preserve the dignity of all human life, from conception to natural death? Invite the apprentices to one of their meetings. Be sure that the horror of abortion is not the only topic, but that the discussion includes the "consistent ethic of life" from conception to natural death.

Christian Formation

Respect for the dignity of all life

◆

Catechetical Resources

Pope John Paul II: *The Gospel of Life*,
   Evangelium Vitae §28, 34, 42, 57,
   58–61, 64–67, 73, 83
CCC §1929–1933, 2258–2301
USCCA pp. 310, 387–402

THE BAPTISM OF THE LORD

Isaiah 40:1–5, 9–11
Comfort, give comfort to my people,
says your God.

Apprenticeship Activity

Consider pairing apprentices with those who bring comfort to the sick and dying through the parish's ministries of care and outreach.

Christian Formation

Extraordinary ministry of the Eucharist, ministry of care

◆

Catechetical Resources

Rite of Anointing and Pastoral Care of the Sick, Introduction
Spiritual and corporal works of mercy
CCC §1500–1510, 2447–2448
USCCA pp. 225–227, 254

LENT

During Lent, if a parish has two "tracks," one for the elect and another for catechumens and candidates who will not celebrate the sacraments until the following year, the following ideas may be used with those bypassing the sacraments. The elect will be on their own journey, preparing for, celebrating, and reflecting upon the celebration of the scrutinies.

FIRST SUNDAY OF LENT

Luke 4:1–13

*Filled with the Holy Spirit, Jesus returned from the Jordan
and was led by the Spirit into the desert for forty days, to be tempted by the devil.
He ate nothing during those days.*

Christian Formation

The discipline of fasting

Catechetical Resources

The U.S. Bishops' Web site has various prayers for those who are fasting: www.usccb.org/nab/fasting.htm
CCC §1434
USCCA pp. 334–335, 518

Apprenticeship Activity

The discipline of fasting has been an important part of the lives of Christians for centuries. Why not choose a particular cause for a week-long fast, such as world peace, respect for the dignity of life, or an end to HIV-AIDS, and invite the apprentices to fast during the week, focusing on one of these causes? Perhaps on one or two days during the week lunch could consist of a simple meal of bread and water. Perhaps people are asked not to eat at a restaurant for the entire week.

SECOND SUNDAY OF LENT

Luke 9:28b–36

*While he was praying his face changed in appearance and
his clothing became dazzling white.*

Christian Formation

Christian art

Catechetical Resources

Books on Christian art, parish stained glass windows, statuary, etc.
CCC §2502–2503

Apprenticeship Activity

Through the centuries artists have depicted numerous scenes in the life of Christ, including the Transfiguration. Is there an art historian or art teacher in the parish who could share images of the Transfiguration with the apprentices?

THIRD SUNDAY OF LENT

Exodus 3:1–8a, 13–15
"Remove the sandals from your feet,
for the place where you stand is holy ground."

Christian Formation

The real presence of Christ in the Eucharist

◆

Catechetical Resources

CCC §1179–1183, 1373–1381
USCCA pp. 174, 219–220, 223–224, 226–227

Apprenticeship Activity

Does the parish church have a chapel or designated area that houses the tabernacle? Invite the apprentices to visit this area for a time of prayer. Since this is "holy ground," consider inviting them to remove their shoes and socks/stockings as they approach the tabernacle for prayer.

FOURTH SUNDAY OF LENT

Luke 15:1–3, 11–32
" 'Father, I have sinned against heaven and against you;
I no longer deserve to be called your son.' "

Christian Formation

Conversion and reconciliation

◆

Catechetical Resources

Rite of Penance, Introduction
CCC §1422–1460, 1848–1876
USCCA pp. 236–237

Apprenticeship Activity

Does the parish have some process to welcome Catholics who have been away from the practice of the faith for some time? If so, invite the apprentices to attend a session for returning Catholics.

FIFTH SUNDAY OF LENT

John 8:1–11

"Let the one among you who is without sin
be the first to throw a stone at her."

Apprenticeship Activity

Capital punishment is one of those "hot button" issues in our society and a topic of special concern for Catholics. Is there someone in the parish or diocese involved in prison ministry–perhaps someone who ministers to those on death row–who could be invited to a session with the apprentices? A discussion about the Church's stance on capital punishment could follow.

Christian Formation

Consistent ethic of life, capital punishment

Catechetical Resources

The U.S. Bishops' Web site contains helpful resources on the topic of capital punishment: www.usccb.org/prolife/issues/cappunish
CCC §2266
USCCA pp. 394–395, 423

PALM SUNDAY OF THE LORD'S PASSION

Luke 22:14 – 23:56

When they came to the place called the Skull, they crucified him.

Apprenticeship Activity

Catholics honor the memory of the crucifixion of Christ in a number of ways. One is to wear a cross or crucifix as a necklace, a lapel pin, or perhaps as a charm on a bracelet. Catholics also place crosses and crucifixes in their cars, at their desks, and in their homes. This might be a good opportunity to visit the various places on the parish property where crosses and crucifixes have been placed. Be sure to research this in advance. Crosses can sometimes be found on parish stationery, on sacred vessels and liturgical books, on vestments, on liturgical linens, on baptismal fonts. Invite the apprentices to lift and carry the parish's processional cross(es).

Christian Formation

The cross of Christ

Catechetical Resources

CCC §616–618
USCCA pp. 91–93, 165–179

EASTER

EASTER TRIDUUM

There is no better way to form people in the Catholic faith than to walk with them through the celebration of the Triduum. Invite them to take part in the washing of feet on Holy Thursday, the veneration of the cross on Good Friday, and the celebration of the initiation sacraments at the Easter Vigil. Invite the apprentices to make this three-day festival a retreat experience.

SECOND SUNDAY OF EASTER

Acts 5:12–16

A large number of people from the towns in the vicinity of Jerusalem also gathered, bringing the sick and those disturbed by unclean spirits, and they were all cured.

Apprenticeship Activity

Invite a Catholic doctor to a session to share his or her experiences of curing people. Consider asking the doctor to share the connecting points between medical practice and faith.

Christian Formation

Care for the sick, Christ the Physician

◆

Catechetical Resources

CCC §1503–1510
USCCA pp. 234–235

THIRD SUNDAY OF EASTER

John 21:1–19
When they climbed out on shore,
they saw a charcoal fire with fish on it and bread.

Apprenticeship Activity

This shoreline breakfast is a sign of the reconciling power of the Eucharist. It is around this meal that Christ reconciles with Saint Peter. Consider planning a barbecue. Invite the apprentices to prepare for this meal by calling to mind people with whom they need to be reconciled. Share these stories around the fire and pray that one day all the world will be reconciled to Christ and that we will be reconciled to one another.

Christian Formation

Conversion and reconciliation

◆

Catechetical Resources

Rite of Penance, Introduction
CCC §1422–1460, 1848–1876
USCCA pp. 236–237

FOURTH SUNDAY OF EASTER

John 10:27–30
Jesus said: "My sheep hear my voice; I know them, and they follow me."

Apprenticeship Activity

Invite your diocesan bishop to a meeting with the apprentices. The neophytes could be invited as well. Be sure to secure the bishop's presence well in advance, since his calendar is probably very full. Invite him to share his experience as the shepherd of the diocese and how his ministry is inspired by the example of Jesus, the Good Shepherd.

Christian Formation

The ministry of the bishop

◆

Catechetical Resources

CCC §1554–1561
USCCA pp. 265–266

FIFTH SUNDAY OF EASTER

Acts 14:21–27

*[Paul and Barnabas] appointed elders for them in each church
and, with prayer and fasting, commended them to the Lord
in whom they had put their faith.*

Apprenticeship Activity

Does your parish or diocese have permanent deacons? There are many possibilities for connecting these men (and their wives) with those in the initiation process. Consider inviting a deacon (and his wife) to a session with the apprentices to share the meaning of diaconal ministry. Or, if a deacon has a particular charism, such as visiting the hospital or visiting the imprisoned, consider pairing an apprentice with a deacon when he "makes his rounds."

Christian Formation

The diaconate

◆

Catechetical Resources

Rites of Ordination, Introduction
CCC §1536–1538, 1543, 1554, 1569–1571
USCCA pp. 264–267, 270–271, 509

SIXTH SUNDAY OF EASTER

Acts 15:1–2, 22–29

*The apostles and elders, in agreement with the whole church,
decided to choose representatives and to send them to Antioch with Paul and Barnabas.*

Apprenticeship Activity

Most (arch)dioceses have a(n) (arch)diocesan pastoral council of some kind that advises the (arch)bishop. Contact your diocesan pastoral center or chancery to see if it is possible for the apprentices to attend one of these pastoral council meetings. This will help them experience the wide array of issues faced by the (arch)diocesan Catholic community.

Christian Formation

(Arch)diocesan church structures

◆

Catechetical Resources

CCC §833
USCCA pp. 113, 115, 133

THE ASCENSION OF THE LORD

Psalm 47:2–3, 6–7, 8–9
Sing praise to God, sing praise.

Apprenticeship Activity

Invite the apprentices to attend a choir rehearsal or invite the parish cantors to a session with the apprentices. Ask them to witness to their great love for music. If your parish has an organ, ask the organist to demonstrate the instrument. If the parish has a large pipe organ, invite the organist to arrange an "organ crawl" with the apprentices.

Christian Formation

Music in Catholic worship

◆

Catechetical Resources

U.S. Bishops: *Music in Catholic Worship, Liturgical Music Today*
CCC §1156–1158
USCCA pp. 171, 175

SEVENTH SUNDAY OF EASTER

John 17:20–26
"Holy Father, I pray not only for them, but also for those who will believe in me through their word, so that they may all be one."

Apprenticeship Activity

Jesus' prayer was that all his followers would be one. Does the parish partner with other Christian denominations in social justice or service projects? Connect apprentices with these efforts.

Christian Formation

Christian unity

◆

Catechetical Resources

Second Vatican Council: *Decree on Ecumenism* §1–12
CCC §820
USCCA p. 128

PENTECOST

John 20:19–23
"Receive the Holy Spirit."

Apprenticeship Activity

Many parishes celebrate the sacrament of confirmation with young people during the Easter season. Invite the apprentices to attend this celebration. Or you may want to invite the confirmation catechists to a session with the apprentices to share their experiences of preparing young people for this sacrament of initiation. Furthermore, those who have been confirmed could be invited to a session to share their experience of preparation for the sacrament. This is a great opportunity to prepare a mystagogical catechesis on the celebration itself with these young people. Do this catechesis at the session with apprentices.

Christian Formation

Sacrament of confirmation

Catechetical Resources

Rite of Confirmation, Introduction
CCC §1285–1321
USCCA pp. 102–110, 201–211

ORDINARY TIME

THE SOLEMNITY OF THE MOST HOLY TRINITY

Psalm 8:4–5, 6–7, 8–9

When I behold your heavens, the work of your fingers.

Apprenticeship Activity

The wonders of creation reveal the splendor of God. Contemplating the beauty of God's creation can lead one to a deeper awareness of God. Too often we simply walk or drive by the wonders of God's creation, barely taking notice. Schedule a visit to a local park, arboretum, forested area, lake, or beach. Invite the apprentices to ponder the beauty of these places. Invite them to pray in thanksgiving for all that God has so wonderfully made for us in this garden of earth.

Christian Formation

God's creation reveals God's presence, respect for God's creation

◆

Catechetical Resources

CCC §341, 2415–2418
USCCA pp. 3–4, 67–68

THE SOLEMNITY OF THE MOST HOLY BODY AND BLOOD OF CHRIST

Psalm 110:1, 2, 3, 4

You are a priest for ever, in the line of Melchizedek.

Apprenticeship Activity

The parish priest is someone who has answered the vocational call to ordained ministry. Invite your priest(s) to a session with the apprentices, not to give a theology of priesthood, but to witness to God's initial and continuing call and how this has been lived out. Invite the apprentices to share their experience of responding to God's call as well. Perhaps a tour of or an open house at the rectory could be arranged.

Christian Formation

Vocation to the priesthood, the priesthood

◆

Catechetical Resources

Rite of Ordination, Introduction
The U.S. Bishops' department on Priestly Life and Ministry has an informative Web site: www.usccb.org/plm
CCC §1546–1553, 1562–1568
USCCA pp. 261–275

SECOND SUNDAY IN ORDINARY TIME

John 2:1–11
There was a wedding at Cana in Galilee.

Apprenticeship Activity

Does the parish have a marriage preparation program? Is there a Pre-Cana program in the area? If so, invite those who minister in these programs to a session with apprentices. Ask them to explain the process as well as witness to God's presence and action in their own marriages. Inspired by the first of Jesus' miracles, perhaps invite the apprentices to share a glass of fine wine during this session!

Christian Formation

Christian marriage

◆

Catechetical Resources

Rite of Marriage, Introduction
CCC §1601–1666
USCCA pp. 277–292

THIRD SUNDAY IN ORDINARY TIME

1 Corinthians 12:12–30
Now you are Christ's body, and individually parts of it.
Some people God has designated in the church to be, first, apostles;
second, prophets; third, teachers; then, mighty deeds; then gifts of healing,
assistance, administration, and varieties of tongues.

Christian Formation

Organization of the parish

Catechetical Resources

Parish mission statement
Parish description of various
    commissions/committees/ministries
CCC §2179
USCCA pp. 121–122, 134–135

Apprenticeship Activity

A parish is a diverse community of people, all with different gifts and talents. The parish council is usually a place where this diversity of gifts is visible. Invite the apprentices to attend a parish council meeting.

FOURTH SUNDAY IN ORDINARY TIME

1 Corinthians 12:31 – 13:13

So faith, hope, love remain, these three; but the greatest of these is love.

Apprenticeship Activity

Think of three people in the parish who embody each of these three virtues. Invite a faith-filled person, a person whose life is imbued with hope, and a person whose love overflows, to a session with the apprentices. These people can witness to the power of these virtues in their lives. They become "living documents" for the apprentices.

Christian Formation

The theological virtues

◆

Catechetical Resources

CCC §1812–1845
USCCA pp. 317, 320, 342–343, 530

FIFTH SUNDAY IN ORDINARY TIME

Luke 5:1–11

When they brought their boats to the shore, they left everything and followed him.

Apprenticeship Activity

Are there vowed religious working on the pastoral staff or residing within the parish? Often, men and women such as these have left everything in order to respond to the Lord's call. Invite one or more of these people to a session to share their vocational experiences.

Christian Formation

Consecrated life

◆

Catechetical Resources

The United States Conference of Catholic Bishops' Department for Consecrated Life provides background materials: www.usccb.org/consecratedlife
CCC §914–933
USCCA p. 135

SIXTH SUNDAY IN ORDINARY TIME

Luke 6:17, 20–26
"Blessed are you who are now weeping, for you will laugh."

Apprenticeship Activity

Does the parish have a ministry to the bereaved? Discuss with the leadership of the bereavement team the possibility of a small number of apprentices attending a meeting. Or invite the bereavement team to a session to talk about the ministry. Perhaps they might be willing to suggest a person who has traveled the journey of grief who can come and speak to the group.

Christian Formation

Grief and bereavement: The Catholic perspective

◆

Catechetical Resources

Order of Christian Funerals,
  Introduction
CCC §1023–1060
USCCA pp. 252–253

SEVENTH SUNDAY IN ORDINARY TIME

Luke 6:27–38
"Love your enemies, do good to those who hate you,
bless those who curse you, pray for those who mistreat you."

Apprenticeship Activity

Unfortunately, the reality of terrorism around the world causes many of us to live in fear for our own safety and the safety of our children. Praying for an end to terrorism and the establishment of a true and lasting peace can help ease our fears and bring an end to this kind of horrible violence. Why not ask the apprentices to create a prayer service for peace and an end to terrorism? Be sure to ask them to formulate prayers for those who are considered enemies. Perhaps members of the liturgy planning committee could assist the apprentices as mentors. All parishioners could then be invited to attend the service.

Christian Formation

Preparing liturgical prayer

◆

Catechetical Resources

Worship preparation materials
  widely available
CCC §2844

EIGHTH SUNDAY IN ORDINARY TIME

1 Corinthians 15:54–58
Therefore, my beloved brothers and sisters, be firm, steadfast,
always fully devoted to the work of the Lord.

Apprenticeship Activity

Often parish staff members make great financial sacrifices in order to dedicate themselves to working for the Church. Their skills would earn more money and benefits in a corporate environment, yet they remain in parish work, devoted to the work of the Lord. Why not arrange for a visit to the offices of the parish staff? Invite apprentices to spend time asking questions, focusing on why a person would choose to become so devoted to the Lord's work for much less compensation than in the "real world."

Christian Formation

Dedication to the work
of the Lord

◆

Catechetical Resources

CCC §2427–2429

NINTH SUNDAY IN ORDINARY TIME

1 Kings 8:41–43
To the foreigner, who is not of your people Israel,
but comes from a distant land to honor you . . .

Apprenticeship Activity

The Church has a long history of ministry to immigrants and refugees. Does your parish or diocese have such a ministry in place? If so, arrange a meeting with those responsible for this ministry. Perhaps invite someone who has immigrated to the United States to share with the group their experience of leaving their homeland to settle in another place.

Christian Formation

Church's solidarity with the
poor and migrants

◆

Catechetical Resources

U.S. Bishops: Pastoral Letter *Economic Justice for All*
Pope John XXIII: *On Christianity and Social Progress*, Mater et Magistra
Pope Paul VI: *The Development of Peoples*, Populorum Progressio
Catholic Relief Services' Web site has excellent resources: www.crs.org
The United States Conference of Catholic Bishops' Department of Migration and Refugee Services provides background materials and action alerts: www.usccb.org/mrs
CCC §1939–1942, 2443–2449
USCCA pp. 420–425, 427–428, 454–456

TENTH SUNDAY IN ORDINARY TIME

Galatians 1:11–19

But when God, who from my mother's womb had set me apart and called me through his grace, was pleased to reveal his Son to me . . .

Apprenticeship Activity

Does the parish or diocese have an active Respect Life group that works to preserve the dignity of all human life, from conception to natural death? Invite the apprentices to one of their meetings. Be sure that the horror of abortion is not the only topic, but that the discussion includes the "consistent ethic of life" from conception to natural death.

Christian Formation

Respect for the dignity of all life

◆

Catechetical Resources

Pope John Paul II: *The Gospel of Life, Evangelium Vitae* §28, 34, 42, 57– 61, 64–67, 73, 83
CCC §1928–1933, 2258–2301
USCCA pp. 43, 337–338, 377–378, 389–402

ELEVENTH SUNDAY IN ORDINARY TIME

Luke 7:36 – 8:3

"When I entered your house, you did not give me water for my feet, but she has bathed them with her tears and wiped them with her hair."

Apprenticeship Activity

Does the parish have an organized ministry of hospitality and welcome? How can we help connect the apprentices to the hospitality ministry of the parish? If people are stationed at the entrances of the parish church to welcome worshipers, why not pair these people with an apprentice before one of the Sunday Masses?

Christian Formation

Aim and purpose of the introductory rites for Mass

◆

Catechetical Resources

General Instruction of the Roman Missal, Introductory Rites
USCCA p. 218

TWELFTH SUNDAY IN ORDINARY TIME

Luke 9:18–24

"If anyone wishes to come after me,
he must deny himself and take up his cross daily and follow me."

Apprenticeship Activity

Often people living with chronic illness become signs of hope and strength, even in the face of constant sickness and pain. These people live with the cross each day of their lives. Invite one or more people living with chronic illness into a session to share their hope and courage with the apprentices.

Christian Formation

Sickness in the Christian context

◆

Catechetical Resources

Rite of Anointing and Pastoral Care of the Sick, Introduction
CCC §1499–1532
USCCA pp. 251–252, 256

THIRTEENTH SUNDAY IN ORDINARY TIME

1 Kings 19:16b, 19–21

The Lord said to Elijah: "You shall anoint Elisha,
son of Shaphat of Abel-meholah, as prophet to succeed you."

Apprenticeship Activity

Invite your parish priest to administer to the catechumens the anointing with the oil of catechumens. Take this opportunity to ask your priest to share with the apprentices the tasks that fill his daily life. How is the parish priest a prophetic witness in today's world? Perhaps this session could include a tour of the parish rectory.

Christian Formation

Oil of catechumens, the priesthood

◆

Catechetical Resources

Rites of Ordination, Introduction
CCC §1539–1554
USCCA p. 185

FOURTEENTH SUNDAY IN ORDINARY TIME

Luke 10:1–12, 17–20
At that time the Lord appointed seventy-two others
whom he sent ahead of him in pairs to every town and place he intended to visit.

Apprenticeship Activity

A great outreach that extends the care of the parish community occurs when someone from the parish brings Communion to someone who is homebound. Consider pairing the apprentices with some of these ministers as they bring Communion to those who are sick and confined.

Christian Formation

Extraordinary ministry of the Eucharist, ministry of care

◆

Catechetical Resources

Rite of Anointing and Pastoral Care of the Sick, Introduction
Spiritual and corporal works of mercy
CCC §1500–1510, 2447–2448
USCCA pp. 225–227, 254

FIFTEENTH SUNDAY IN ORDINARY TIME

Luke 10:25–37
"But a Samaritan traveler who came upon him
was moved with compassion at the sight."

Christian Formation

Pastoral care of the sick

◆

Catechetical Resources

Rite of Anointing and Pastoral Care of the Sick, Introduction
CCC §1499–1532
USCCA p. 256

Apprenticeship Activity

Too many people in nursing homes and long-term care facilities have too few visitors. Contact the person in charge of visitors at one of these facilities and arrange for your apprentices to spend time with the residents.

SIXTEENTH SUNDAY IN ORDINARY TIME

Luke 10:38–42

Jesus entered a village where a woman whose name was Martha welcomed him.

Apprenticeship Activity

Does the parish have an organized ministry of hospitality and welcome? How can we help connect the apprentices with the hospitality ministry of the parish? If people are stationed at the entrances of the parish church to welcome worshipers, why not pair these people with an apprentice before one of the Sunday Masses? If the parish regularly schedules coffee and snacks following the weekend liturgies, ask that the apprentices take a turn preparing and serving at this time of hospitality.

Christian Formation

Christian hospitality and welcome

◆

Catechetical Resources

Pope Paul VI: *The Development of Peoples*, Populorum Progressio §67–69

General Instruction of the Roman Missal, Introductory Rites

SEVENTEENTH SUNDAY IN ORDINARY TIME

Luke 11:1–13

"And I tell you, ask and you will receive;
seek and you will find; knock and the door will be opened to you."

Apprenticeship Activity

Prayer of petition is at the heart of the prayer life of the Christian. Invite the apprentices to express their deep needs and longings. Urge them to formulate these into prayers of petition. Perhaps those who compose the parish's general intercessions for Mass could be invited to share their gift for writing with the apprentices. At the end of the session, use the composed prayers as a closing prayer.

Christian Formation

Prayer of petition

◆

Catechetical Resources

CCC §2629–2633
USCCA pp. 467–468, 485–490, 493–494

EIGHTEENTH SUNDAY IN ORDINARY TIME

Psalm 90:3–4, 5–6, 12–13, 14, 17

If today you hear his voice, harden not your hearts.

Apprenticeship Activity

Invite some of the parish lectors to a session with the apprentices. Ask them to share their love for the scripture and how the word inspires them in their daily lives. Perhaps the session could include a trip into the church. Invite the lectors to show and explain how biblical readings are organized into the Lectionary for Mass. Perhaps the apprentices could be invited to proclaim a reading from the Lectionary at the ambo.

Christian Formation

The word of God

◆

Catechetical Resources

U.S. Bishops: *Fulfilled in Your Hearing: The Homily in the Sunday Assembly*
Lectionary for Mass, Introduction
CCC §2653–2655
USCCA pp. 175, 177, 218

NINETEENTH SUNDAY IN ORDINARY TIME

Luke 12:32–48

"Sell your belongings and give alms."

Apprenticeship Activity

Invite the apprentices to organize a garage sale. Encourage them to go to their clothes closets and collect everything that has not been worn in one year. Invite them to take an honest inventory of their household possessions with an eye toward keeping those "things" that are essential, and setting aside items for the sale. All of the items could then be collected, perhaps at the home of one of the apprentices, or perhaps on the parish property. Schedule the garage sale, and be sure that people know that all proceeds will be donated to the parish or to a specific ministry or charity sponsored by the parish.

Christian Formation

Church's solidarity with the poor

◆

Catechetical Resources

Pope Leo XIII: *The Condition of Labor,* Rerum Novarum §28–30
Pope John XXIII: *On Christianity and Social Progress,* Mater et Magistra §159–160
Pope Paul VI: *The Development of Peoples,* Populorum Progressio §43, 44, 51, 57, 61, 73, 76
John Paul II: *On Social Concern,* Sollicitudo Rei Socialis §17
Catholic Relief Services' Web site has excellent resources: www.crs.org
CCC §1939–1942, 2443–2449
USCCA pp. 420–425, 427–428, 454–456

TWENTIETH SUNDAY IN ORDINARY TIME

Hebrews 12:1–4
Since we are surrounded by so great a cloud of witnesses . . .

Apprenticeship Activity

Statues of saints have always played an important part in the faith lives of believers. Does your church building, or perhaps an older church in your area, contain saints' statues? Schedule a tour of the statuary in your church or another one. Find the names of the saints portrayed in the statuary and ask the apprentices to research those saints' lives before the visit. Ask the apprentices to share the information as you stand at the statue. Be prepared to pray a prayer asking that the particular saint intercede on behalf of the needs of all present.

Christian Formation

Communion of saints, statuary

◆

Catechetical Resources

Lives of the saints
U.S. Bishops: *Built of Living Stones: Art, Architecture, and Worship*
CCC §946–948, 1674
USCCA pp. 160–161, 220, 507

TWENTY-FIRST SUNDAY IN ORDINARY TIME

Psalm 117:1, 2 (Mark 16:15)
"Go out to all the world and tell the Good News."

Apprenticeship Activity

Does the parish have an evangelization committee? If so, ask members to share their experiences with the apprentices. In turn, invite the apprentices to the work of evangelization by sharing with members of the committee the joy they have found in the Good News of Jesus Christ. Consider inviting them to a meeting of this parish committee.

Christian Formation

Evangelization

◆

Catechetical Resources

Pope Paul VI: *On Evangelization in the Modern World*, Evangelii Nuntiandi
Pope John Paul II: *The New Evangelization*
U.S. Bishops: *Our Hearts Were Burning Within Us: A Pastoral Plan for Adult Faith Formation in the United States*
USCCA pp. 16–17, 134–136, 502

TWENTY-SECOND SUNDAY IN ORDINARY TIME

Luke 14:1, 7–14

*"Rather, when you hold a banquet, invite the poor, the crippled, the lame,
the blind; blessed indeed will you be because of their inability to repay you."*

Apprenticeship Activity

Is there a soup kitchen or homeless shelter in the community that regularly serves meals to the needy? Contact the organization and arrange for the apprentices to serve one of those meals.

Christian Formation

Church's solidarity with the poor

◆

Catechetical Resources

U.S. Bishops: Pastoral Letter *Economic Justice for All* §174–178, 181, 182, 185, 188, 192

Pope Leo XIII: *The Condition of Labor,* Rerum Novarum §28–30

Pope John XXIII: *On Christianity and Social Progress,* Mater et Magistra §159, 160

Pope Paul VI: *The Development of Peoples,* Populorum Progressio §43, 44, 51, 57, 61, 73, 76

John Paul II: *On Social Concern,* Sollicitudo Rei Socialis §17

Catholic Relief Services' Web site has excellent resources: www.crs.org

CCC §1939–1942, 2443–2449

USCCA pp. 420–425, 427–428, 454–456

TWENTY-THIRD SUNDAY IN ORDINARY TIME

Philemon 9–10, 12–17

*I, Paul, an old man, and now also a prisoner for Christ Jesus, urge you on behalf of my child Onesimus,
whose father I have become in my imprisonment; I am sending him, that is, my own heart, back to you.*

Apprenticeship Activity

The love expressed by Saint Paul on behalf of his child Onesimus is captured in his calling his son his "own heart." This is the kind of love that holds Catholic families together as well. Does the parish have a family life ministry? Do they schedule Catholic family events? Invite the apprentices to one of these events or invite the family life leaders to a session.

Christian Formation

Catholic family life

Catechetical Resources

CCC §2204–2233

USCCA pp. 373–385

TWENTY-FOURTH SUNDAY IN ORDINARY TIME

Luke 15:1–32

" 'But now we must celebrate and rejoice, because your brother was dead and has come to life again; he was lost and has been found.' "

Apprenticeship Activity

Addictions often cause the addicted person to become "lost." Do you know of someone in the parish who has successfully recovered from an addiction and who can witness to the power of God in his or her transformation? Invite that person to a session with the apprentices.

Christian Formation

Conversion

◆

Catechetical Resources

Rite of Penance, Introduction
CCC §1427–1429, 1848–1876
USCCA pp. 235–237

TWENTY-FIFTH SUNDAY IN ORDINARY TIME

Luke 16:1–13

"You cannot serve both God and mammon."

Apprenticeship Activity

Giving of our treasure is a foundational pillar of living the life of a good steward. Does the parish have a stewardship committee? Invite a member of that committee to witness to the power of stewardship. Invite the apprentices to a meeting of the parish finance committee so that they can see firsthand the needs of the parish and the difference their own stewardship can make.

Christian Formation

Stewardship

◆

Catechetical Resources

U.S. Bishops: *Our Hearts Were Burning Within Us: A Pastoral Plan for Adult Faith Formation in the United States* §71, 122
The International Catholic Stewardship Council has excellent resources on its Web site: www.catholicstewardship.org
USCCA pp. 450–455

TWENTY-SIXTH SUNDAY IN ORDINARY TIME

Luke 16:19–31

"He said, 'Then I beg you, father, send him to my father's house, for I have five brothers, so that he may warn them, lest they too come to this place of torment.' "

Apprenticeship Activity

Jesus is very clear in the Gospel. If we ignore the needs of the poor while being absorbed in our own riches, the consequences are dire. Arrange a visit to a homeless shelter. Ask the staff of the shelter if the apprentices might be able to assist there one evening.

Christian Formation

Hell

◆

Catechetical Resources

CCC §1033–1041
USCCA pp. 153–156

TWENTY-SEVENTH SUNDAY IN ORDINARY TIME

Luke 17:5–10

The apostles said to the Lord, "Increase our faith."

Apprenticeship Activity

Contact the parish director of religious education to arrange for a visit of the apprentices to a religious education class for young children. Perhaps the apprentices could be assigned to take part in teaching the class. Sharing from their own new experience of the faith, this session just might lead them to a future of ministry to children of the parish!

Christian Formation

The teaching office of the Church

◆

Catechetical Resources

General Directory for Catechesis
U.S. Bishops: *Our Hearts Were Burning Within Us: A Pastoral Plan for Adult Faith Formation in the United States*
CCC §94–95, 426–429
USCCA pp. 133, 330

TWENTY-EIGHTH SUNDAY IN ORDINARY TIME

Luke 17:11–19

As he was entering a village, ten lepers met him.

Apprenticeship Activity

Contact your diocesan Catholic Charities office and find out about the many services they offer to those in the community who are considered outcasts. Seek ways to connect apprentices with these ministries of help and outreach.

Christian Formation

Solidarity with the poor and the outcast

◆

Catechetical Resources

U.S. Bishops: Pastoral Letter *Economic Justice for All*
CCC §1939–1942, 2046,
   2443–2449
USCCA pp. 420–425, 427–428,
   454–456

TWENTY-NINTH SUNDAY IN ORDINARY TIME

2 Timothy 3:14 – 4:2

*All Scripture is inspired by God and is useful for teaching, for refutation,
for correction, and for training in righteousness.*

Christian Formation

The Bible, the word of God

◆

Apprenticeship Activity

Is there a Bible study group that meets at your parish or one nearby? Invite the apprentices to one of its meetings.

Catechetical Resources

U.S. Bishops: *Fulfilled in Your Hearing:
   The Homily in the Sunday Assembly*
Lectionary for Mass, Introduction
CCC §81, 2653–2655
USCCA pp. 26–27

THIRTIETH SUNDAY IN ORDINARY TIME

2 Timothy 4:6–8, 16–18
I have competed well; I have finished the race; I have kept the faith.

Apprenticeship Activity

Invite an elderly member of your parish to come to a session to share with the apprentices his or her own story of steadfastness in faith over the years. Perhaps invite someone who has been through many hardships–possibly the death of a spouse–and has remained faithful through it all.

Christian Formation

Persistence in prayer, faith in the midst of trials

◆

Catechetical Resources

Lives of the saints
CCC §2729–2731
USCCA pp. 476–480

THIRTY-FIRST SUNDAY IN ORDINARY TIME

Luke 19:1–10
Now a man there named Zacchaeus,
who was a chief tax collector and also a wealthy man,
was seeking to see who Jesus was.

Christian Formation

Evangelization

◆

Apprenticeship Activity

Is there anyone currently inquiring about the Catholic faith in your parish? In other words, are there people in the precatechumenate stage of Christian initiation? Invite them to come to a session with the apprentices. Surface their questions and invite the apprentices to witness to the power of Christ in their own lives.

Catechetical Resources

Pope Paul VI: *On Evangelization in the Modern World, Evangelii Nuntiandi*
Pope John Paul II: *The New Evangelization*
U.S. Bishops: *Our Hearts Were Burning Within Us: A Pastoral Plan for Adult Faith Formation in the United States*
USCCA pp. 16–17, 134–136, 502

THIRTY-SECOND SUNDAY IN ORDINARY TIME

2 Maccabees 7:1–2, 9–14

*It happened that seven brothers with their mother were arrested
and tortured with whips and scourges by the king,
to force them to eat pork in violation of God's law.*

Apprenticeship Activity

Many Catholic organizations work for the rights of those unjustly arrested and tortured around the world. Catholic Relief Services is one such organization. Is there a CRS representative in your parish or diocese? Invite that person to a session with the apprentices. Perhaps a letter-writing campaign could begin as a way to address the issues of torture and injustice.

Christian Formation

Torture and injustice

◆

Catechetical Resources

Catholic Relief Services' Web site has excellent resources: www.crs.org
CCC §2297–2298
USCCA p. 311

THIRTY-THIRD SUNDAY IN ORDINARY TIME

Psalm 98:5–6, 7–8, 9

*Sing praise to the LORD with the harp,
with the harp and melodious song.
With trumpets and the sound of the horn
sing joyfully before the King, the LORD.*

Apprenticeship Activity

Are there parishioners who assist in the music ministry of the parish by playing an instrument? Invite them to a session with the apprentices. Ask them to share what it means for them to give of their talent to the parish. If some of the apprentices play a musical instrument, invite them to bring it to this session. Perhaps they can be given some of the liturgical music used in the parish. They could then learn it and begin ministering to the apprentices and to the wider worshiping assembly during the Liturgy of the Word at Sunday Mass.

Christian Formation

Music in Catholic worship

◆

Catechetical Resources

U.S. Bishops: *Music in Catholic Worship, Liturgical Music Today*
CCC §1156–1158
USCCA pp. 171, 175

THIRTY-FOURTH OR LAST SUNDAY IN ORDINARY TIME
THE SOLEMNITY OF OUR LORD JESUS CHRIST THE KING

Luke 23:35–43

"Amen, I say to you, today you will be with me in Paradise."

Apprenticeship Activity

It is fitting at the end of the liturgical year to spend time pondering the beginning and the end of our lives. Is there someone in the parish who cares for people who are in the last stages of life? Invite that person to a session with the apprentices. Invite them to share their experiences from the perspective of belief in the afterlife, in the kingdom of heaven.

Christian Formation

Heaven

◆

Catechetical Resources

CCC §1023–1029
USCCA pp. 153–159

INDEX OF TOPICS

This alphabetical listing of catechetical topics provides another way to find the material in this book. Look up the topic that you are interested in, and find the Sunday with an apprenticeship activity related to that topic. Then you can turn to that Sunday for the resources you need.

SUNDAYS AND TOPICS AT A GLANCE

LITURGICAL YEAR A

ADVENT/CHRISTMAS

First Sunday of Advent – Catholic social teaching on peace and justice
Second Sunday of Advent – Aim and purpose of the introductory rites for Mass
Third Sunday of Advent – Church's solidarity with the poor
Fourth Sunday of Advent – Dignity of the human person; solidarity with those in crisis
Christmas – Church's commitment to care for the poor
The Holy Family of Jesus, Mary, and Joseph – Dignity of the human person, especially the elderly
The Solemnity of the Blessed Virgin Mary, the Mother of God – Marian devotion
The Epiphany of the Lord – Christian unity
The Baptism of the Lord – Church's ministry to the poor

LENT

First Sunday of Lent – Church as the sacrament of reconciliation
Second Sunday of Lent – Conversion and reconciliation
Third Sunday of Lent – Sacrament of baptism
Fourth Sunday of Lent – Church's ministry of healing
Fifth Sunday of Lent – Funerals, Christian death, resurrection of the body
Palm Sunday of the Lord's Passion – Stations of the Cross, paschal mystery

EASTER

Second Sunday of Easter – Catholic social teaching on peace and justice
Third Sunday of Easter – Preaching the gospel of Christ
Fourth Sunday of Easter – Christ is the Good Shepherd
Fifth Sunday of Easter – Sacrament of holy orders
Sixth Sunday of Easter – The Christian virtue of hope
The Ascension of the Lord – Music in Catholic worship
Seventh Sunday of Easter – The role of women in the Church
Pentecost – Sacrament of confirmation

ORDINARY TIME

The Solemnity of the Most Holy Trinity – The Trinity, Catholic family life
The Solemnity of the Most Holy Body and Blood of Christ – The liturgy
Second Sunday in Ordinary Time – Sacrament of reconciliation
Third Sunday in Ordinary Time – The priesthood
Fourth Sunday in Ordinary Time – Grief and bereavement
Fifth Sunday in Ordinary Time – Church's solidarity with the poor
Sixth Sunday in Ordinary Time – Conversion and reconciliation
Seventh Sunday in Ordinary Time – Forgiveness of enemies
Eighth Sunday in Ordinary Time – Stewardship
Ninth Sunday in Ordinary Time – The catechetical ministry of the Church: Sharing the tradition
Tenth Sunday in Ordinary Time – Conversion and reconciliation
Eleventh Sunday in Ordinary Time – Catholic health care
Twelfth Sunday in Ordinary Time – Evangelization
Thirteenth Sunday in Ordinary Time – The cross, paschal mystery
Fourteenth Sunday in Ordinary Time – Christian death
Fifteenth Sunday in Ordinary Time – Preaching the gospel of Christ
Sixteenth Sunday in Ordinary Time – Prayer
Seventeenth Sunday in Ordinary Time – Christian art
Eighteenth Sunday in Ordinary Time – Church's solidarity with the poor
Nineteenth Sunday in Ordinary Time – Prayer

Twentieth Sunday in Ordinary Time – Ecumenism
Twenty-first Sunday in Ordinary Time – The ministry of the bishop
Twenty-second Sunday in Ordinary Time – The cross, paschal mystery
Twenty-third Sunday in Ordinary Time – Extraordinary ministry of the Eucharist, ministry of care
Twenty-fourth Sunday in Ordinary Time – Forgiveness and the sacrament of reconciliation
Twenty-fifth Sunday in Ordinary Time – The Mass in the life of the Catholic
Twenty-sixth Sunday in Ordinary Time – Organization of the parish
Twenty-seventh Sunday in Ordinary Time – Conversion and reconciliation
Twenty-eighth Sunday in Ordinary Time – Grief and bereavement: The Catholic perspective
Twenty-ninth Sunday in Ordinary Time – Stewardship
Thirtieth Sunday in Ordinary Time – The virtue of Christian hospitality
Thirty-first Sunday in Ordinary Time – Prayer
Thirty-second Sunday in Ordinary Time – Adoration of the Blessed Sacrament
Thirty-third Sunday in Ordinary Time – Christian marriage
Thirty-fourth or Last Sunday in Ordinary Time: Solemnity of Our Lord Jesus
    Christ the King – Church's solidarity with the poor

LITURGICAL YEAR B

ADVENT/CHRISTMAS
First Sunday of Advent – Small Christian communities
Second Sunday of Advent – Conversion and reconciliation
Third Sunday of Advent – Church's solidarity with the poor
Fourth Sunday of Advent – Dignity of human life, Christian motherhood
Christmas – Church's solidarity with the poor and migrants
The Holy Family of Jesus, Mary, and Joseph – Consecrated life
The Solemnity of the Blessed Virgin Mary, the Mother of God – Dignity of human life, Christian motherhood
The Epiphany of the Lord – Stewardship
The Baptism of the Lord – The word of God

LENT
First Sunday of Lent – Contemplative prayer
Second Sunday of Lent – Persistence in prayer, faith in the midst of trials
Third Sunday of Lent – "I am the Lord, your God": The Ten Commandments
Fourth Sunday of Lent – Corporal works of mercy: Burying the dead
Fifth Sunday of Lent – The cross of Christ
Palm Sunday of the Lord's Passion – Holy oils, anointing of the sick

EASTER
Second Sunday of Easter – Church's solidarity with the poor
Third Sunday of Easter – Catholic social teaching on peace and justice
Fourth Sunday of Easter – The ministry of the bishop
Fifth Sunday of Easter – Parish as community of believers
Sixth Sunday of Easter – Christian marriage
The Ascension of the Lord – The teaching office of the Church
Seventh Sunday of Easter – Vocation to the priesthood, the priesthood
Pentecost – Sacrament of confirmation

ORDINARY TIME
The Solemnity of the Most Holy Trinity – Sacrament of baptism
The Solemnity of the Most Holy Body and Blood of Christ – The parish church and its furnishings
Second Sunday in Ordinary Time – Vocation to the priesthood, the priesthood
Third Sunday in Ordinary Time – The teaching office of the Church

Fourth Sunday in Ordinary Time – Music in Catholic worship
Fifth Sunday in Ordinary Time – Care for the sick
Sixth Sunday in Ordinary Time – Solidarity with the poor and the outcast
Seventh Sunday in Ordinary Time – Holy oils, anointing of the sick
Eighth Sunday in Ordinary Time – The discipline of fasting
Ninth Sunday in Ordinary Time – The virtue of Christian hospitality
Tenth Sunday in Ordinary Time – Sacrament of baptism, original sin
Eleventh Sunday in Ordinary Time – God's creation reveals God's presence, respect for God's creation
Twelfth Sunday in Ordinary Time – Preparing liturgical prayer
Thirteenth Sunday in Ordinary Time – Church's ministry of healing
Fourteenth Sunday in Ordinary Time – Sickness in the Christian context
Fifteenth Sunday in Ordinary Time – Christian hospitality, welcome, forming community
Sixteenth Sunday in Ordinary Time – Contemplative prayer
Seventeenth Sunday in Ordinary Time – Church's solidarity with the poor
Eighteenth Sunday in Ordinary Time – Reception of the Holy Eucharist
Nineteenth Sunday in Ordinary Time – The Eucharist
Twentieth Sunday in Ordinary Time – Music in Catholic worship
Twenty-first Sunday in Ordinary Time – Christian marriage
Twenty-second Sunday in Ordinary Time – The word of God
Twenty-third Sunday in Ordinary Time –The languages of the liturgy
Twenty-fourth Sunday in Ordinary Time – Church's solidarity with the poor
Twenty-fifth Sunday in Ordinary Time – Catholic social teaching on peace and justice
Twenty-sixth Sunday in Ordinary Time – Marriage tribunal, canon law
Twenty-seventh Sunday in Ordinary Time – The teaching office of the Church
Twenty-eighth Sunday in Ordinary Time – Prayer
Twenty-ninth Sunday in Ordinary Time – Church's solidarity with the poor
Thirtieth Sunday in Ordinary Time – Church's ministry of healing
Thirty-first Sunday in Ordinary Time – Dignity of the human person, especially the elderly
Thirty-second Sunday in Ordinary Time – Stewardship
Thirty-third Sunday in Ordinary Time – Oil of catechumens, the priesthood
Thirty-fourth or Last Sunday in Ordinary Time: The Solemnity of Our Lord Jesus
    Christ the King – Persistence in prayer, faith in the midst of trials

LITURGICAL YEAR C

ADVENT/CHRISTMAS
First Sunday of Advent – The content of the Catholic faith
Second Sunday of Advent – Evangelization
Third Sunday of Advent – Church's solidarity with the poor
Fourth Sunday of Advent – Dignity of human life, Christian motherhood
Christmas – Church's solidarity with the poor and migrants
The Holy Family of Jesus, Mary, and Joseph – Dignity of human life, Christian motherhood
The Solemnity of the Blessed Virgin Mary, the Mother of God – Wonder at God's creation
The Epiphany of the Lord – Respect for the dignity of all life
The Baptism of the Lord – Extraordinary ministry of the Eucharist, ministry of care

LENT
First Sunday of Lent – The discipline of fasting
Second Sunday of Lent – Christian art
Third Sunday of Lent – The real presence of Christ in the Eucharist
Fourth Sunday of Lent – Conversion and reconciliation
Fifth Sunday of Lent – Consistent ethic of life, capital punishment
Palm Sunday of the Lord's Passion – The cross of Christ

EASTER
Second Sunday of Easter – Care for the sick, Christ the Physician
Third Sunday of Easter – Conversion and reconciliation
Fourth Sunday of Easter – The ministry of the bishop
Fifth Sunday of Easter – The diaconate
Sixth Sunday of Easter – (Arch)diocesan church structures
The Ascension of the Lord – Music in Catholic worship
Seventh Sunday of Easter – Christian unity
Pentecost – Sacrament of confirmation

ORDINARY TIME
The Solemnity of the Most Holy Trinity – God's creation reveals God's presence, respect for God's creation
The Solemnity of the Most Holy Body and Blood of Christ – Vocation to the priesthood, the priesthood
Second Sunday in Ordinary Time – Christian marriage
Third Sunday in Ordinary Time – Organization of the parish
Fourth Sunday in Ordinary Time – The theological virtues
Fifth Sunday in Ordinary Time – Consecrated life
Sixth Sunday in Ordinary Time – Grief and bereavement: The Catholic perspective
Seventh Sunday in Ordinary Time – Preparing liturgical prayer
Eighth Sunday in Ordinary Time – Dedication to the work of the Lord
Ninth Sunday in Ordinary Time – Church's solidarity with the poor and migrants
Tenth Sunday in Ordinary Time – Respect for the dignity of all life
Eleventh Sunday in Ordinary Time – Aim and purpose of the introductory rites for Mass
Twelfth Sunday in Ordinary Time – Sickness in the Christian context
Thirteenth Sunday in Ordinary Time – Oil of catechumens, the priesthood
Fourteenth Sunday in Ordinary Time – Extraordinary ministry of the Eucharist, ministry of care
Fifteenth Sunday in Ordinary Time – Pastoral care of the sick
Sixteenth Sunday in Ordinary Time – Christian hospitality and welcome
Seventeenth Sunday in Ordinary Time – Prayer of petition
Eighteenth Sunday in Ordinary Time – The word of God
Nineteenth Sunday in Ordinary Time – Church's solidarity with the poor
Twentieth Sunday in Ordinary Time – Communion of saints, statuary
Twenty-first Sunday in Ordinary Time – Evangelization
Twenty-second Sunday in Ordinary Time – Church's solidarity with the poor
Twenty-third Sunday in Ordinary Time – Catholic family life
Twenty-fourth Sunday in Ordinary Time – Conversion
Twenty-fifth Sunday in Ordinary Time – Stewardship
Twenty-sixth Sunday in Ordinary Time – Hell
Twenty-seventh Sunday in Ordinary Time – The teaching office of the Church
Twenty-eighth Sunday in Ordinary Time – Solidarity with the poor and the outcast
Twenty-ninth Sunday in Ordinary Time – The Bible, the word of God
Thirtieth Sunday in Ordinary Time – Persistence in prayer, faith in the midst of trials
Thirty-first Sunday in Ordinary Time – Evangelization
Thirty-second Sunday in Ordinary Time – Torture and injustice
Thirty-third Sunday in Ordinary Time – Music in Catholic worship
Thirty-fourth or Last Sunday in Ordinary Time: The Solemnity of Our Lord Jesus Christ the King – Heaven